THE VICTORIA HISTORY OF HAMPSHIRE

BASINGSTOKE:
A MEDIEVAL TOWN, *c.*1000–*c.*1600

John Hare

First published 2017

A Victoria County History publication

© The University of London, 2017

ISBN 978-1-909646-61-2

INSTITUTE OF HISTORICAL RESEARCH | SCHOOL OF ADVANCED STUDY UNIVERSITY OF LONDON

Typeset in Minion Pro by Jessica Davies Porter

CONTENTS

LIST OF ILLUSTRATIONS

All photography by John Hare unless otherwise stated.

LIST OF MAPS AND TABLES

FOREWORD

For those of us who study the history of England the Victoria County History is a distinguished, dependable and longstanding friend. Yet it is not stuck in its ways. The great red books, ranging over the landscape parish by parish, have been joined by newer projects. This volume is part of that renaissance and Merton College is delighted to have been able to assist in its publication.

The college's links with Basingstoke are old and various. Our founder Walter de Merton, chancellor of King Henry III and bishop of Rochester, was born in the town and founded a hospital there, which for many years cared for sick fellows of the college as well as aged local residents. As a result some of the key documents for Basingstoke's medieval history are still kept in the college archives. In the fifteenth and sixteenth centuries our neighbours play their part in the story too, Magdalen College as patron of the parish church and Corpus Christi College as the study destination for sons of the town's leading citizens. More recently we were able to welcome John Hare to Merton for a term's visit in support of his earlier research.

The beauty of the VCH is that in exploring in detail the history of individual communities it sheds unique light on the history of England as a whole. Basingstoke emerges from this study as a classic centre of the booming late medieval cloth industry. Large flocks of sheep grazed the fields outside the town and weavers worked in the villages around. Mercers and drapers, dyers and fullers ran the town and built fine timber-framed buildings, a few of which survive to this day. Collectively they reconstructed the parish church in impressive style and steered the Holy Ghost guild through the Reformation by converting it into a school trust.

Yet the men and women of Basingstoke were not just anonymous examples of larger trends and here they emerge in all their individuality, letting their pigs wander in the wrong places, emptying their dyeing vats into the river at the wrong times, buying and selling Mediterranean spices and deep sea fish, objecting for very understandable reasons when the vicar built his privy over the common washing stream. As work progresses on succeeding volumes of the history of Basingstoke and on similar projects, the Hampshire VCH is clearly in flourishing health and we wish it every success in the years ahead.

Steven Gunn

Steven Gunn
Professor of Early Modern History,
Merton College, Oxford

MERTON COLLEGE
OXFORD

ACKNOWLEDGEMENTS

THIS TEXT IS THE THIRD of the 'shorts' published by the new Victoria County History of Hampshire which aims to rewrite the Hampshire VCH volumes, formerly published in the first two decades of the 20th century in accordance with the changing demands of a century later. The first two volumes covered nearby villages (Mapledurwell and Steventon). This is the first to deal with the town of Basingstoke, a town with a distinguished, albeit often forgotten, historical heritage, but which was transformed at the end of the last century. It is hoped that this book will be of interest both to a Basingstoke audience and to historians interested in the small towns of medieval England.

This volume possesses a single authorship, but I have benefitted from the support and enthusiasm of the VCH volunteer group, who have been working on the history of the area, and have provided a constant reminder that each single volume is part of a wider and interconnecting study, both geographically and chronologically. The group's valuable work on the neighbouring villages and the more modern town is accessible on the VCH website.[1] The book has also greatly benefitted from the support of specific individuals. Dr Jean Morrin has kept the whole project going and read and commented on the complete text. The work of the wills group has made the Basingstoke 17th century wills and inventories accessible on the VCH website, and Dr Karen Parker, who has been producing transcripts of those for the town in the 16th century, made these accessible to me, prior to their eventual appearance on the web. With regards to the buildings I have been dependent on discussions with Bill Fergie, Edward Roberts and Richard Warmington. Professor Robert Swanson has kindly shared his work on Gosmer, and Dr Rebecca Oakes provided me with a list of the town's recruits to Winchester College. Most of the relevant records are carefully looked after by the Hampshire Record Office and I am grateful to the staff there for their consistent support. I have also appreciated the help of the archivists at Merton College and Magdalen College Oxford, Julian Reid and Robin Darwall-Smith, whose institutions were both landowners in the medieval town. Finally, any author on this subject must be thankful for the work of our 19th predecessors, Baigent and Millard, with their publication of many original documents.

The VCH Hampshire project is dependent on the support and grants from a variety of organisations, funds and individuals. Most recently these have included donations from Professor Jim and Mrs Mary Anne Wilkes, The Hackwood Arts Trust, and the Hampshire Field Club and Archaeological Society. We are most grateful for all support, whether great or small. The County Trust of the VCH has paid for the maps. The Warden and Fellows of Merton College Oxford have provided a grant towards the publication

1 'Hampshire Work in Progress': https://www.victoriacountyhistory.ac.uk/counties/hampshire/work-in-progress (accessed 8 Nov. 2017); 'VCH Explore': https://www.victoriacountyhistory.ac.uk/explore (accessed 8 Nov. 2017).

of this volume. This is greatly appreciated, as is Professor Steven Gunn's readiness to provide a foreword on their behalf.

The following individuals and organisations must be thanked for the use of their images: Bill Fergie, Bob Applin, Mary Oliver, Derek Spruce, The Hampshire Cultural Trust, The Hampshire Record Office and The National Trust.

The support of VCH central office at the Institute of Historical Research (University of London) has been essential and much appreciated, initially from Richard Hoyle, and in carrying this volume through to publication: Adam Chapman, Lianne Sherlock and Jessica Davies Porter. Cath D'Alton produced the maps.

John Hare
November 2017

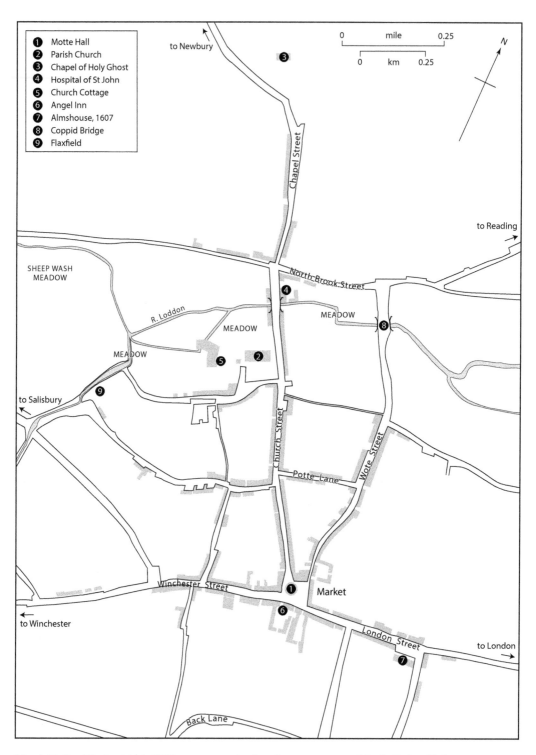

Legend:
1. Motte Hall
2. Parish Church
3. Chapel of Holy Ghost
4. Hospital of St John
5. Church Cottage
6. Angel Inn
7. Almshouse, 1607
8. Coppid Bridge
9. Flaxfield

to Newbury

to Reading

mile 0 0.25

km 0 0.25

N

SHEEP WASH MEADOW

North Brook Street

Chapel Street

R. Loddon

MEADOW

MEADOW

MEADOW

MEADOW

to Salisbury

Church Street

Wote Street

Potte Lane

Winchester Street

to Winchester

Market

London Street

to London

Back Lane

Map 1 *Medieval Basingstoke (c.1500): a reconstruction based on a map prepared for the Duke of Bolton in 1762.*

Growth and Development of the Town, *c.*1000–*c.*1600

The Emergence of the Town

BASINGSTOKE POSSESSES A long and rich history that goes back to before the Norman Conquest. Although, overshadowed by the greater and richer towns of Winchester and Southampton it was, during this period and afterwards, one of the major urban centres in Hampshire. For a long time it served as the market centre for north-east Hampshire, providing consumer goods and necessities for the surrounding villages, and a market for their own agricultural produce. In addition, it became a major stopping centre on the road from London to the west. Finally, it also became an important manufacturing centre for national and international trade, as it did in the 15th and 16th centuries for cloth, and in the latter part of the 19th century for engineering and clothing.

Basingstoke grew up on the edge of the valley of the river Loddon which cuts into the northern edge of the chalk down.[1] It thus incorporated the great chalk downlands (which in the Middle Ages and afterwards were noted for large-scale sheep farming) as well as the meadow, valley and nearby clay soils. The origins of the town probably lie in one of many settlements dependent on the royal manor of Basing. Its first documented reference is in 990, when meadowland at Basingstoke was included in a royal grant.[2] Its location was well suited to trade, where the main east–west route along the northern edge of the chalklands was crossed by routes going north from the south coast towards Reading and the Thames valley, and north-west to Newbury and the river Kennet, and was joined by the route from Southampton and Winchester.

Basingstoke's name suggests that it was a subordinate settlement of Basing or the Basingas[3] and it had probably emerged as a town by the time of Domesday Book in 1086, when it was in royal possession. It was then one of the few centres in the county recorded as possessing a market, in this case valued at 30*s.*, suggesting the presence of some form of specialist trading.[4] It was a large settlement or group of settlements with 20 villans (*villani*), 8 bordars (*bordari*), 12 coliberts (*coliberti*), and 6 slaves (*servi*). There was land for 20 ploughs suggesting that there was already a substantial settlement or group of

---

1   British Geological Survey, Solid and Drift edn, 284 Basingstoke (1981).

2   P.H. Sawyer, *Anglo-Saxon Charters* (London, 1968), 289; H.P.R. Finberg, *The Early Charters of Wessex* (Leicester, 1964), 59.

3   R. Coates, *The Place Names of Hampshire* (London, 1989), 29. Variant spellings include Basingstoke, Basingstock, Basingstoch, Basingestoch, Basingestok, Bassingestoke.

4   *Domesday*, 93.

settlements. There were three mills and woodland for 20 pigs.[5] In the Pipe roll of 1167–8, it paid £8 13*s.* 4*d.* in aid, or royal tax, a substantial figure, but, as in the Domesday entry, it was valued at less than Alton, which was subsequently an important but lesser town.[6] Significantly the surrounding unit of jurisdiction, the hundred, was already known as that of Basingstoke, and not named after that of the mother church or settlement of Basing, suggesting that the subordinate settlement was already well-established.

The town had probably grown out of a group of valley settlements represented by the settlement around the parish church, by Eastrop (now absorbed by the town) and by a possible settlement on the river's north bank. The market probably lay on the site of the market square, to the south of these settlements and on the high ground, where it was adjacent to the natural main route from London towards the south-west, now represented by London Street and Winchester Street. As the town grew these various elements were linked together in a single settlement, and in a compact complex of streets on both sides of the river Loddon (see below, Maps 1 and 3). The medieval town's main public buildings included the parish church, the town hall or Mote (in the market place and documented from 1389), the chapel of the Holy Ghost (by 1244), and the hospital of St John (from 1240s), with a major almshouse being added at the beginning of the 17th century. Otherwise the townscape would have been dominated by timber-framed one or two storeyed houses. The town also remained an agricultural community, the compressed urban centre being surrounded until 1788 by its open fields. Institutionally, the town achieved early self-government under the crown. By about 1200, there is clear evidence that the crown had devolved responsibility to the townsmen (see below). Ecclesiastically, it and Basing remained part of a single parish, in the hands successively of Mont St Michel (Dept. Manche, France), Selborne Priory (Hants) and Magdalen College, Oxford. Since the rector was, for almost the whole of the period, an absentee ecclesiastical institution, the town's more important churchman was the vicar, who was appointed in turn by the priory and the college (see below, pp. 77–8).

Markets and Fairs

Small towns like Basingstoke depended on markets and trade as much as the larger and more important towns. Agricultural produce from the surrounding area was effectively exchanged for consumer goods, and specialist manufactures or services. This could take place in the market, the fair, shops or in the informal places for trade such as the inns. This interaction between the country and the town took place throughout this period but it is only in the 15th century that it became better documented (see below). Basingstoke possessed a market from the time of Domesday and this continued, albeit changing the day from Sunday to Monday in 1203 and to Wednesday in 1214. There are other early references to markets in 1234 and 1267–8, and it continued in 2017.[7] In 1449 the town acquired a fair by royal grant. Most fairs long preceded this, and this grant may have reflected the growing prosperity and ambitions of the town. It was to be held around the chapel of the Holy Ghost, a prominent feature of urban life, and this may also suggest the

5   *Domesday*, 93.
6   *Pipe R* 1167–8 (PRS 11), 181–2.
7   S. Letters, *Gazetteer of Markets and Fairs in England and Wales to 1516*, I (List and Index Soc., Kew, 2003), 151; *Cal. Chart.* VI, 107.

initiative of the town lay behind this grant. A second fair is mentioned in 1622, but is not known from any other source.[8]

Despite the fragmentary nature of the evidence, Basingstoke grew in the 12th and 13th century, and was part of a much wider urban growth in England during this period. By the end of the 13th century, it had clearly emerged as one of the main regional centres of Hampshire. Thus it had the sixth highest assessment in the county in the taxation of 1334, and the same ranking among the tax-payers of 1327 (Table 1). Already, in the 12th and early 13th centuries, it figured prominently in the aids and tallages paid to the king, where Andover, Basingstoke and Alton were the main towns after Winchester and Southampton. Contemporaries perceived the town to be important. It sent MPs to parliament in 1295, 1302 and 1306, although this subsequently ceased.[9] It was important enough to appear, albeit represented as a single building, on the highly selective Gough map in the 14th century.[10] It became far more important than the former ecclesiastical mother church of Basing which, in the 13th century, became a dependent chapel of the new town.[11] We know little of the town's trade. Much of it would have been of local transactions that linked the town and the nearby villages: the agricultural producers and the urban craftsmen. The presence of such craftsmen and specialisms is reflected in occasional surnames in the 1327 tax assessments.[12] But we also gain occasional glimpses of its long-distance trade: as in the export of wool through Southampton, where large-scale trading is recorded in 1270s (see below, p. 47).[13]

Appropriately this growing importance was reflected in the emergence to national history of a few citizens of the town. The most notable was Walter of Merton or, as he would originally have been known, Walter of Basingstoke or Basing. Walter came from a well-established family of Basingstoke free-holders. He received education in the hands of Merton Priory (Surr.) and took its name thereafter. He made the shift to royal service and rose within this. He was a royal clerk, who became a major minister. Rewarded with the bishopric of Rochester, his career reached its peak as Chancellor, one of the most important posts in royal government. In the long run, he became most noted as founder of Merton College, Oxford. Although he made his career outside the town of his birth, it remained important to him: he was concerned with the education of his many nephews; and that recruitment to his college should prioritise those from within the diocese of Winchester; he founded a hospital in the town and he ordered that if he died in Hampshire he would be buried in Basingstoke's parish church next to his parents.[14] Walter's contemporary, John of Basingstoke (d. 1252), was also a scholar, educated at the University of Paris and spent time studying in Constantinople. He was also known to the monastic chronicler, Matthew Paris and to the bishop of Lincoln, Robert Grosseteste.[15]

8   Letters, *Gazetteer of Markets and Fairs*, I, 151.

9   Baigent & Millard, *Basingstoke*, 77, 316, 339.

10   *Bodleian Libr., MS Gough Gen. Top. 16*: http://www.goughmap.org/settlements/8087 (accessed 5 Jan. 2017).

11   Macray, *Selborne* I, 8–14; II, 16–18.

12   *Hants Tax List 1327*, 70–1; below.

13   *Cal. Pat.* 1266–72, 555, 689; 1272–81, 36; Baigent & Millard, *Basingstoke*, 185.

14   ODNB, s.v. Merton, Walter of (*c*.1205–77), administrator, bishop of Rochester, and founder of Merton College, Oxford (accessed 5 Jan. 2017); J.R.L. Highfield (ed.), *The Early Rolls of Merton College, Oxford* (Oxford Hist. Soc., 1964), 9.

15   ODNB, s.v. Basingstoke, John of [John Basing] (d. 1252), scholar and ecclesiastic (accessed 5 Jan. 2017).

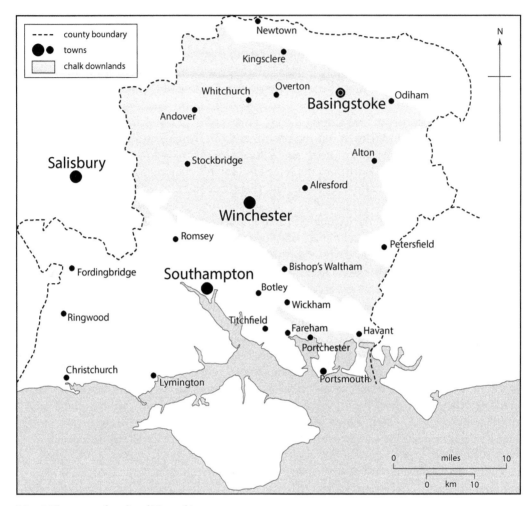

Map 2 *The towns of medieval Hampshire.*

Families also established themselves as prominent figures in London. Adam of Basing (*c*.1220–66) a rich merchant, alderman and mayor was an important supplier to Henry III, particularly of very expensive embroidery and vestments, silks and other luxuries, including many gifts to churches.[16] Between 1238 and 1260 he was paid the vast sum of £2,514 for goods purchased by Henry III.[17] Although he was described as 'of Basing', he would have gone to London when Basingstoke was regarded as part of the parish of Basing.[18] Other merchants and citizens of London included more than one Thomas de Basing, a son of Adam (fl. 1265–70) and a son of Walter of Basing (fl. 1271).[19]

16   *Cal. Lib.* 1245–51, *passim*; 1251–60, 218, 516, 517; A.F. Sutton, *The Mercery of London: trade, goods and people, 1130–1578* (Aldershot, 2005), 29.

17   Sutton, *Mercery of London*, 29.

18   See below, 78.

19   Sutton, *Mercery of London*, 35; *Cal. Pat.* 1266–72, 554.

Thomas de Basing (fl. 1270, 1272 and 1293) and William de Basing (dead by 1319) were wool traders.[20]

Unfortunately, we have virtually no information on what would have been the most cataclysmic blow to Basingstoke, and other medieval towns, the Black Death of 1348–9 which here, as elsewhere, probably wiped out about half the population of the town. Moreover, the records of the poll tax of 1377, which elsewhere provide a valuable source of information about relative population sizes, rarely survive for Hampshire and not at all for Basingstoke. On a more limited scale the town was struck by a major conflagration in 1392.

	Population			Taxable wealth		S'oton trade
	1327	1524/5	1603	1334	1524/5	1430–1540
	Taxpayers	Taxpayers	Communicants	Assessment (£)	Assessment (£)	Carts
1	Winchester (197)	Southampton* (268)	Southampton (2138)	Winchester (51)	Southampton	
2	Southampton (139)	Winchester (596)	Winchester (1851)	Southampton (51)	Winchester	Winchester (2332)
3	Ringwood (77)	Basingstoke (316)	Romsey (1317)	Ringwood (22)	Basingstoke (69)	Romsey (705)
4	Andover (70)	Alton (260)	Christchurch (1236)	Andover (20)	Alton (55)	Andover (279)
5	Lymington** (68)	Romsey (210)	Ringwood (1199)	Portsmouth (13)	Ringwood (23)	Basingstoke (173)
6	Basingstoke (66)	Andover (152)	Basingstoke (1000)	Basingstoke (12)	Andover (22)	Alton (152)
7	Portsmouth (62)	Portsmouth (124)	Andover (872)	Lymington (10)	Odiham (21)	Ringwood (121)
8	Romsey (55)	Odiham (113)	Fordingbridge (833)	Romsey (8)=	Romsey (20)	Alresford (107)
9	Titchfield (46)	Bishop's Waltham (102)	Alton (700)	Titchfield (8)=	Alresford (17)=	Fordingbridge (8)
10	New Alresford (34)	Ringwood (100)	Overton (552)	Alton (5.5)	Portsmouth (17)=	Hursley (8)

Table 1 *The ranking of Hampshire towns. Sources: Hants Tax List 1327; Reg. Distr. Wealth 1524–5; Dioc. Pop. Retns; Glasscock (ed.), Subsidy 1334, 106–21; Overland Trade Database.*

* The number of taxpayers for Southampton is incomplete and excludes the two richest parishes. The precise ranking of Winchester and Southampton is thus speculative.
** New and Old Lymington have been included together.

These figures must be treated with caution. Each column is based on different criterion, and tax assessments were by their very nature full of problems. They provide at least a sense of contemporary perceptions. The number of communicants in Basingstoke of exactly 1,000 suggests an approximation, but the table does make clear that Basingstoke was one of the most important towns in the county and that it rose in importance between the 14th and the 16th centuries.

20 Sutton, *Mercery of London*, 140; *Cal. Pat.* 1266–72, 689; E. Eckwell (ed.), *Two Early London Subsidy Rolls* (Lund, 1951), 53, 168, 62, 248.

Nevertheless, the town recovered from these traumas and prospered in the 15th century – and especially in the later 15th and early 16th centuries – when it reached the peak of its medieval and early modern prosperity. The town's increasing regional importance is seen in the growth of its trade with Southampton and the increasing number of carts that went direct to the town, seen through the exceptional evidence of the Brokage Books of Southampton which recorded all the carts leaving Southampton and their destinations.[21]

By the early 16th century (in 1524/5), Basingstoke had become one of the more important towns of England: 55th in the ranking by taxable population and 51st by wealth.[22] It had only half the population of Winchester, but its assessment was three-quarters of that of this former capital of England. It might only have risen from sixth to the third wealthiest town in Hampshire, but it had far overtaken Andover, Portsmouth and Ringwood (which had previously surpassed it), and it now had an assessment over twice that of Portsmouth, the next highest in that group.[23]

Basingstoke retained its importance as a market centre for the area around and as a place on the major route from Salisbury and the West Country to London. Moreover, this route probably increased in importance with the rising commercial activity of both Salisbury and London. The importance of the route could be recognised by government as in 1406 when a grant of pavage was made for three years to spend on the highway between Hartford Bridge and Basingstoke, the main route to London as it crossed the clay lands east of the town. Significantly the two supervisors were the parson of Newnham (a local man) and a leading Salisbury merchant, Richard Spencer.[24] Basingstoke's importance on this vital national route from London to Salisbury was recognised by Shakespeare and the royal post (a system for the distribution of royal messages around the country).[25]

But it was, above all, the growth of the cloth industry in the town and in the surrounding villages that generated Basingstoke's increased wealth and population. In the late 14th and 15th centuries, England shifted from being an exporter of wool to one of manufactured cloth. This expansion generated both jobs and surpluses for consumption. Basingstoke lay at the heart of one area of this growing textile industry among the small towns of north Hampshire, such as Odiham and Overton, and above all Alton (which rose to national importance and to the fourth most important town in Hampshire in 1524/5) as well as in the surrounding villages. As the textile economy grew so did the number of craftsmen who were required to cater for the new prosperity and the needs of the town. Something of the impact of this growing industry will be seen throughout this book. However, in the 17th century the industry was in decline (see below, p. 37).

---

21   J. Hare, 'Southampton's trading partners: the small towns of Hampshire and Wiltshire', *English Inland Trade*, 95–7.
22   A. Dyer, 'Ranking lists of English medieval towns', *CUHB*, 747–70; *Reg. Distr. Wealth 1524–5*, ii, 117–37. National rankings like local ones need to be treated with caution since they may be measuring in different ways and some records are missing, but behind the apparent exactitude lies a useful approximation of a town's position.
23   A. Dyer, 'Ranking lists of English medieval towns', *CUHB*, 747–70; *Reg. Distr. Wealth 1524–5*, ii, 117–37.
24   *Cal. Pat.* 1405–8, 267.
25   Shakespeare, *Henry IV*, part I, II.1; M. Brayshay, 'The royal pack-horse routes of Hampshire in the reign of Elizabeth I', *PHFC* 48 (1992), 123, 133.

Townscape and Buildings

When the Duke of Tuscany visited the town on the way from Salisbury to London in 1669, his secretary wrote in his diary, 'The town, which is wretched, both in regard to the buildings, the greater part of which are in wood, and the total absence of trade'.[26] This is probably the earliest description of the medieval houses of the town. It is likely that the town had already experienced decline and difficulties, and the buildings lacked the brick and stucco of fashionable buildings elsewhere. Like so many buildings in the area, they would have been timber-framed, on stone footings, with wattle and daub infill to the framing, but it would be wrong to see them as 'wretched': they were instead a frequent reminder of the town's prosperity a century before, and of its carpenters, although the timber-framed tradition continued in this region well into the latter part of the 17th century.[27] Stone buildings were exceptional: the parish church, the chapel of the Holy Ghost and some of the buildings of the hospital of St John are the only known such buildings (see below, chapter 5), and they were surrounded by a townscape of one or two-storey timber-framed houses. Something of the available building materials can be seen in the accounts for the hospital of St John. Here the timber structures were raised on low stone footings. Flints were collected from the fields around and carted in, and only few buildings were probably stone throughout. Buildings were thatched or tiled; thus in 1346/7, a barn was roofed with straw but tiles were used on the hall and on the chapel in 1364/5.[28] Bricks were used here by the 1490s.[29] Tiles were used to roof the Holy Ghost chapel in the late 16th century.[30]

But for us, making sense of what the town would have looked like, is made more difficult by subsequent rebuilding, and particularly the transformation of the 1960s, when, after a period of decay, much of the site of the medieval town, its streets and any surviving medieval remains were swept away to create a new shopping centre and related buildings. This was the most dramatic and extensive example of a long process of piecemeal replacement or redevelopment that had taken place over the previous centuries, whether as a result of the accidental periodic fires or subsequent urban growth as in the 19th century. In 1889, Baigent and Millard, the town's historians, had commented, 'change and decay are rapidly removing the few lingering relics of old street architecture in the Town'.[31] It was the scale of the 1960s redevelopment that was different.

Fortunately, this new and massive shopping centre did not extend to the higher part of the town, where lay the main medieval route from London to Winchester, Salisbury and the West Country, together with the town's market place. Even in this upper town, piecemeal redevelopment and replacement had taken place, albeit not involving the wholesale destruction seen elsewhere. It provides us with the classic High Street of a market town, containing buildings of all ages, from the Middle Ages to the present. In some cases, owners wanted to bring their buildings up to date, in other cases, as with the 19th-century London Street chapel, to give the site a totally different function. In

26 Baigent & Millard, *Basingstoke*, 80.
27 Roberts, *Hampshire Houses*, chapters 8 and 9.
28 Merton Coll., 4356, 4357.
29 Merton Coll., 4363.
30 Millard, *Holy Ghost*, passim.
31 Baigent & Millard, *Basingstoke*, 561.

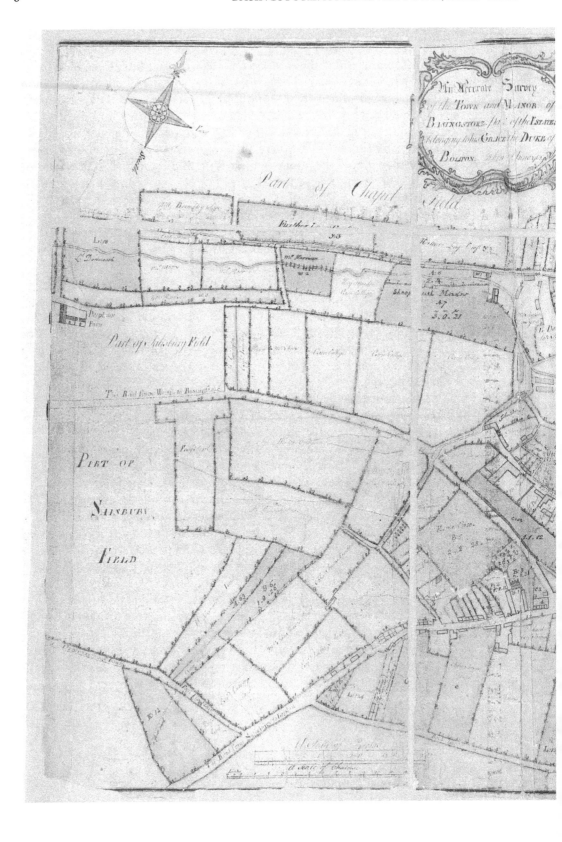

Map 3 *Basingstoke in 1762: a map prepared for the Duke of Bolton.*

Figure 1 *Market Place, showing the main road to London and the 16th-century town hall, in the early 19th century.*

addition, buildings had to survive the dangers of fire which periodically swept through parts of these timber-framed streets. One occurred in 1392, and another in about 1656.[32] Moreover, the dangers continued. On one side of Winchester Street running up to New Street lies a distinctive row of early-20th century shops built to replace those burnt down in the fire of 1905. Photographs of Thomas Burberry's shop before the fire suggest that this included jettied timber-framed buildings, that had later been refaced but were probably of medieval or 17th-century date. Nevertheless, we cannot be sure of the dating, since this type of construction continued beyond 1600 until the later 17th century.

It should be emphasised that this bustling middle-sized town was small by modern standards. The townsman could walk from one end of the town to the other in about five minutes, as long as a conversation could be avoided on the way. To those who know Basingstoke today, most of the historic town lay within the footprint of the modern shopping centre. Only around the church and in the area of the market place and the main east–west street did the medieval town extend and survive beyond this.

We can at least establish the street pattern of the medieval town, parts of which still survive particularly in the upper town, from a detailed map of 1762. Although this comes from a later date, the intervening centuries were not a period of growth, so that the map together with earlier occasional documentation allow an approximate reconstruction on of the scale and street plan of the medieval town (Maps 1 and 3). At the top of the hill, was a rectangular market place which projected from the line of the main road

32   Baigent & Millard, *Basingstoke*, 75, 78–9, 685.

Figure 2 *The topography of the town: Church Street rising to meet the market place and the main London road (2016).*

from Winchester to London (London Street and Winchester Street). It was originally larger than that today since encroachments are recorded from the 13th century.[33] Encroachments may also have occurred subsequently, whether documented or still visible as in the former Anchor public house in London Street.[34] Within the market place was the Mote Hall, or town hall, which had a stall or shop beneath.[35] It is documented from 1389.[36] The market was originally larger than at present with the museum (formerly town hall) built on part of it.

Running down from the market square were two streets which led to bridges over the river Loddon. Church Street, which with the parish church probably represented the earliest settlement, led to the road to Newbury, via a north bank suburb, Whiteway (*c.*1250), or Chapel Street (1542), and the Holy Ghost chapel. A group of timber-framed buildings survived on this street until the 1960s.[37] The regularity of the tenement sizes in the 18th century, in the upper part of Church Street suggests that this may represent

33   Baigent & Millard, *Basingstoke*, 183.
34   Baigent & Millard, *Basingstoke*, 286 for 1461; B. Fergie, 'The former Anchor public house, London Street, Basingstoke', *HFC Newsletter* 58 (2012), 17.
35   Baigent & Millard, *Basingstoke*, 382, 383.
36   Baigent & Millard, *Basingstoke*, 213, with repairs, or the need for repairs, recorded on 316, 339, 347.
37   Photo by D. Wren in HRO, 146A12.

an early planned expansion of the town. Further east, Oat Street or Wote Street (1507, 1508, 1556) led to Coppid bridge and the road to Reading. Crossing these downward streets were cross streets, such as Potters Lane (Potte Lane 1473), Cross Street part way down, and Brook Street on the other side of the river Loddon.[38] At the river itself there were both the bridges,[39] some of the industrial buildings that required water (with at least two dyeworks), as well as the hospital of St John, which lay on the north side of the river. Both main roads rose steeply from the valley floor to the market square, which would have generated problems in wet weather, dealt with on Church Street by the construction of a causeway, presumably for pedestrians, from the Angel Inn on Winchester Street to Church gate.[40] The streets were narrow and sometimes cases were brought against citizens for blocking them. Bridges also needed to be repaired.

There are few surviving medieval houses. The earliest seems to be on London Street (the former Anchor public house) whose roof structure suggests an early date, now reinforced by Carbon 14 dating. It can probably be dated to the first quarter of the 14th century, making it one of the four earliest dated crown post roofs in Hampshire.[41] This early building was set back from the present road, with a later building lying between it and the street frontage. This suggests the presence of continued encroachment, such as had earlier occurred in the 13th century and after, both in the market place and on an unspecified royal route.[42] On the opposite side of London Street, there is a group of timber-framed houses some with jetties cut back and refronted in the 19th century (nos 23, 25, 25a, 26, 26a) (Fig. 3).[43] Here, at least, there was no subsequent encroachment since these medieval houses, some with jetties cut back, are on line with the rest of the north side of the street. Nevertheless, we should envisage the distinct possibility of London Street having originally been a much broader market street.

The medieval inns, as later, were concentrated around the market, London Street and Winchester Street, as still seen in 1762 (Figs 1 & 3). Laarsens (formerly the Feathers), at the top of Wote Street, provides the remnants of one such courtyard inn with the north range incorporating 16th-century building. The main half-timber front, however, dates from the later 17th century.[44] Just outside our period are the almshouses set up under the 1608 will of one of the town's most successful London merchants, James Deane, and which fully survive along London Street.[45]

---

38   The dates for the streets are the earliest known dates taken from J.E. Gover, *Hampshire Place Names* (typescript 1961), copy on shelves in HRO.

39   Baigent & Millard, *Basingstoke*, 312.

40   HRO, 5M52/C1; 148M71/8/5/2.

41   B. Fergie, 'The former Anchor public house', 17. It possesses a crown post/collar purlin roof. This suggests a much earlier date than the 18th/19th century given by NHL, no. 1230863, Flintz/The Anchor Inn and Hants HER 2127 (both accessed 8 Feb. 2017). C14 dating provides an 89.4 per cent probability of it being built between 1300 and 1326 (Oxford Radiocarbon Accelerator Unit C14/4780). I am grateful to Dr Martin Bridge, Edward Roberts and Bill Fergie for these dates and discussion on them and on the building itself, and to Hampshire Field Club, Historic Buildings Section and Hampshire Building Survey group for financing the dating.

42   Baigent & Millard, *Basingstoke*, 245, 48, 73, 84, 86, 245, 286, 294, 308, 354.

43   NHL, no. 1092591, 23, 25, 25A, London Street, and no. 1264317, 26, 26A, London Street (accessed 8 Feb. 2017).

44   E. Roberts, *The Feathers Inn Basingstoke: an architectural history and report* (typescript HRO B1/A202/1–7); NHL, no. 1092589, The Feathers Public House (accessed 8 Feb. 2017).

45   Baigent & Millard, *Basingstoke*, 588; NHL, no. 1339724, Deane's Almshouses (accessed 8 Feb. 2017).

Figure 3 *Medieval houses in London Street with surviving jetty. The house on the left is of similar date but the jetty has been subsequently cut back and replaced with the surviving decorated pattern.*

Away from this main medieval road, there are a few surviving buildings. At Cross Street there is a small collection of early two-storey houses. The rather grander corner building with a jettied gable on Church Street is 16th-century but extensively restored.

Church Cottage lower down into town, but outside the 1960s redevelopment, shows some of the building activity of the early 16th century, and represents the house of a wealthy merchant (Figs 4 & 5).[46] In about 1527, a large new two-storeyed extension was added on to the existing, now lost, main house. It is far too large to have been a domestic service wing, and probably represented one of the shops or workshops in which the finishing of cloth took place, and which are recorded in many inventories. The existing domestic house was then replaced by a new elaborate and expensive house, with an integral chamber over the hall, in 1541–2.[47] In 2017, its lavish timber framing and fine quality ashlar chimney stack still reflect the wealth of its owner.

Although little survives of the houses of the medieval town itself, more can be seen from comparison with the houses of other north Hampshire towns which themselves saw much rebuilding in the 15th and 16th centuries.[48] This can be supplemented by the

46   NHL, no. 1230694, Church Cottage (accessed 8 Feb. 2017).
47   B. Fergie and M. Oliver, 'Dates from dendrochronology at Church Cottage, Basingstoke', *HFC Newsletter* 47 (2007), 19–23; M. Oliver, *Church Cottage, Basingstoke: Historical notes* (Basingstoke, 2007), 6–11. The dating in the text is based on dendrochronological evidence. See also Roberts, *Hampshire Houses* (new edn, 2016), 287, 288, 303.
48   See Roberts, *Hampshire Houses*, chapters 8 and 9; J. Hare, 'Regional prosperity in fifteenth-century England: some evidence from Wessex', in M. Hicks (ed.), *Revolution and Consumption in Late Medieval England* (Woodbridge, 2001), 112–13.

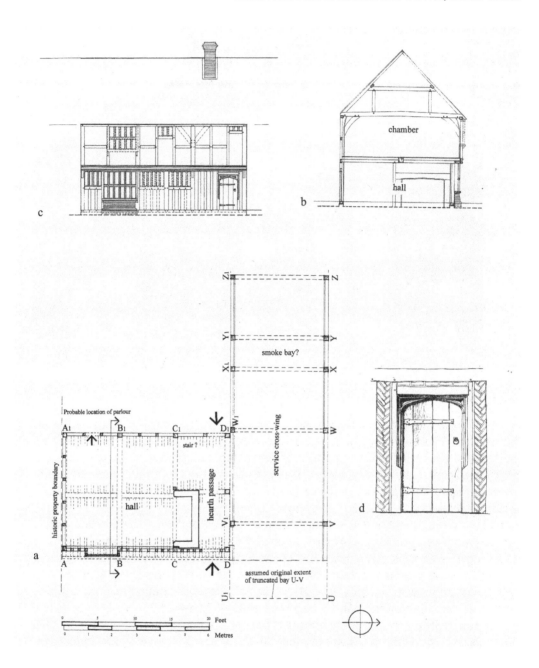

Figure 4 *Church Cottage showing the mixture of house and workshop so frequently found in the inventories and among the houses of clothiers at this time in Basingstoke. [An early building has now disappeared, but the large service wing (U– Y) is dated using tree ring evidence, to 1527 and was extended (Y-Z) in 1537/8. The new hall and hearth passage replaced the earlier one and are dated 1541/2, see also b, c, d.]*

Figure 5 *Church Cottage (2017). The lavish decoration of the central timber framed portion of 1541/2, and the fine ashlar of the interior chimney stack reflect the wealth of Basingstoke's traders. The portion on the right has been truncated (see Fig. 4) and represents a plainer earlier industrial range.*

evidence of later 16th-century inventories, which recorded the goods of the dead person as part of the whole process of dealing with the will. Those drawing up the inventories were interested in contents and furnishings rather than in the houses themselves, and the records of rooms are incidental details, and sometimes omitted. They give us information about the better-off people within the town, yet even among the surviving inventories there would be considerable variation in the rooms provided. At one extreme were the houses of the very rich, and Thomas Lane, the rich mercer, whose wide range of goods in his shop is examined elsewhere (below, p. 50), may be taken as an example of one such large house. Lane had a shop; hall; chamber over the hall; chamber over the shop; chamber over the street door; a garret; a study; an entry between the hall and the kitchen; kitchen; yelling house (for brewing); backside (or courtyard); warehouse and a malt loft.[49] At the other extreme were small houses with a hall, chamber and kitchen.[50] There were some elements that were standard in the inventories. There was a hall, usually a chamber above the hall (for the days when the hall was open to the roof had now gone),[51] parlour and kitchen. The entrance to the property was recorded, but only if there happened to be a room above. Occasionally there was a cellar.[52] There were rooms associated with business, mostly to do with the cloth industry, and these show something of what was going on. These clothier's shops, or workshops, seem to have been concerned with

---

49   HRO, 1532B/09.
50   A. Hawker, *Voices of Basingstoke* (Basingstoke, 1983), 23.
51   Roberts, *Hampshire Houses, 1250–1700*, 148–9.
52   HRO, 1554B/110; 1571B/193; 1575B/74; 1580AD/48; 1588AD/148; 1598AD/48.

quality control, looking after the final finishing of the cloth and repairs of any faults, with tables, shears and boulting irons. There were other buildings specifically related to particular trades. There were wool stores,[53] and dyehouses.[54] A few other specific occupations are also recorded as with a baker with his bakehouse and a chamber over the bread shop[55] or a cobbler's shop.[56] Finally, the urban farms remind us of the presence of agriculture in the town.[57]

53   HRO, 1598AD/71; 1554B/110.
54   HRO, 21M65/D3/43.
55   HRO, 1588AD/48.
56   HRO, 1588AD/48.
57   e.g. the wealthy Roger Ryve, HRO, 1575B/74.

LAND AND GOVERNMENT

Landownership

THE TOWN WAS already a royal possession in Domesday Book in 1086 where it was described as always having been a royal manor.[1] It remained effectively a single manor, which achieved self-government under the crown. One likely exception was the land that Walter of Merton had given to St John's hospital, and became a possession of Merton College Oxford, and probably became the manor of Water Martyn. This was evidently perceived by some contemporaries as a distinct manor in 1541, when presentments were made against those carrying bread and ale out of the manor of Water Martens, thus presumably hoping to avoid the fine due from producers in the town's own jurisdiction where the goods were sold.[2] Merton College clearly regarded it as a separate manor.[3] Other accumulations of land may also have later claimed the title, as seen in a reference to the manor of Taulkes belonging to John Hall, gentleman in 1633.[4] In the Middle Ages, it was the townsmen as a corporate body, rather than a single lord, who were in charge and to whom the tenants paid rent and owed responsibility.

The rent that was paid was recorded in surviving rentals and these show considerable variation within the rents; some people held many tenements which they then sublet whereas others held just a single tenement.[5] The 1521 rental shows something of this varied pattern of land holding.[6] There were the noble and gentry outsiders: the lords of Basing, the prior of Merton, the heirs of the Brocas family (of the neighbouring Beaurepaire manor) and Robert Wallop, another neighbouring lord. There was Richard Gosmer, who, as vicar, was a major tenant within the town, and the house (or hospital) of St John. Then there were the rich families of the town itself, whose names will become familiar in later chapters. Above all there was John Kingsmill, although by this stage the family had become outsiders to the town, who held ten properties. There was John Bowyer with eight, John Belchamber and Thomas Canner (in 1521 an academic outsider) with four and James Deane with three. Other names included cloth dealers like Bye, Lancaster, Locker and Stocker. Such patterns of landholding were subject to change. Winchester College bought property in the town in 1468 and 1480.[7] Most dramatic was the sale of the Kingsmill holdings to William Paulet, the lord of Basing in 1540. John II

1   *Domesday*, 93.
2   Baigent & Millard, *Basingstoke*, 333.
3   Merton Coll., 4341, 4342, 4350; H.E. Salter, *Registrum annalium collegii Mertoniensis 1483–1521* (Oxford Hist. Soc., 1923), 142.
4   Baigent & Millard, *Basingstoke*, 201.
5   Baigent & Millard, *Basingstoke*, 378–90.
6   HRO, 148M71/3/1/10.
7   Himsworth, *Winchester Coll.* II, 83, 86, 179.

who sold up these properties was son of the John who had been Justice of the Common Pleas and grandson of Richard Kingsmill,who had been the richest innkeeper in the 15th century, was probably already a migrant from the town.[8] John's decision to sell his urban properties was probably associated with the need for cash to acquire ex-monastic land in the same year and set himself as a proper country landowner.[9] However, the transactions also remind us of the workings of the urban land market. The documents include a listing of the year's rent received by Kingsmill, and this reflects how dramatically higher was the rent that he received from his tenants than that which he paid to the town.[10]

Local Government

Basingstoke gradually acquired the element of self-government under the crown. By about 1200, there is clear, but fragmentary, evidence of the townsmen running their own affairs in return for a fixed annual payment direct to the royal exchequer. In 1174 a reeve of the town is referred to, and again in 1204/5.[11] In 1212 the town was required to provide the king with soldiers, one of only four towns in Hampshire to do so.[12] In 1237, the bailiffs of Basingstoke were cited before the justices concerning a £20 loan.[13] The crown also delegated some legal responsibilities, the town being represented by its own jury in 1236.[14] It was freed from the sheriff's interference in 1241 and possessed return of writs in 1256 and 1275.[15] The crown delegated to the town the responsibility of finance and paying its annual rent, or fee farm, to the royal exchequer as in 1211/2,[16] 1225,[17] 1228,[18] 1230,[19] 1256.[20] Occasionally the figure was changed, thus it was lowered in 1226 from £82 12*s.* to £72 12*s.*, but raised in 1256, depending on how many of the surrounding hundreds, or legal districts, were included in the fee farm.[21] Nevertheless, in troubled times, as in the early 13th century, this would not be a permanent settlement. Occasionally the king took the town in hand as in 1220 and 1228[22] and sometimes the king granted the fee farm to one of his followers as in 1216 and 1247.[23] This emerging self-government and independence under the crown seems to have become firmly established with the charter granted by the king to the men of the town in 1256.[24] This

8   See below, 67–8 , 73.
9   HRO, 19M61/6–9. He bought Sydmonton together with some other land at a cost of £976, *L & P Hen VIII*, XV, 1540, 290–1.
10   HRO, 19M61/9; 148M71/3/1/10.
11   *Pipe R* 1174–5 (PRS 22), 194; 1204–5 (PRS 57), 129.
12   Baigent & Millard, *Basingstoke*, 65.
13   Baigent & Millard, *Basingstoke*, 66–7.
14   M.W. Beresford and H.P.R. Finberg, *English Medieval Boroughs: a Handlist* (Newton Abbot, 1973), 118.
15   *Cal. Chart.* VI, 107.
16   Baigent & Millard, *Basingstoke*, 362.
17   Baigent & Millard, *Basingstoke*, 68.
18   *Cal. Chart.* I, 68; *Cal. Fine HIII* II, 189.
19   *Cal. Chart.* I, 68; *Cal. Fine HIII* II, 330.
20   *Cal. Chart.* I, 453.
21   *Cal. Chart.* I, 68; IV, 121; Baigent & Millard, *Basingstoke*, 364–5.
22   *Cal. Fine HIII* I, 141–2.
23   *Cal. Chart.* IV, 14; *Cal. Pat.* 1216–26, 104, 247.
24   *Cal. Chart.* IV, 121.

Figure 6 *Market hall from Titchfield, built c.1620 providing a suggestion of what that at Basingstoke might have looked like. The Titchfield example was re-erected and restored to an approximation of its original appearance, at the Weald and Downland Living Museum in 1974.*

charter was also seen as the basis for their privileges and was confirmed subsequently in 1329, 1414 and 1449.[25] It established that in return for a fixed payment direct to the exchequer, the men of the town would have freedom of toll throughout the country, the right to judge their own internal debt cases and that royal writs should go through them. This independence was seen in practice in a grant of 1256 to Walter of Merton.[26] Subsequently the royal income from the town might be granted to a member of the royal family or other beneficiary, as in 1269, when it was granted to Queen Eleanor.[27] These changes reflected the growing importance of the town, as did the decision to include it in the summons to parliament in 1295, 1302 and 1306.[28]

In 1392, the townsmen made use of a heavy fire to secure a new charter making the townsmen a perpetual community with a common seal.[29] Physically, its independence was reflected by its town hall or Motte Hall, which existed in the market place by 1389,

25   *Cal. Chart.* IV, 121; *Cal. Pat.* 1413–16, 204; *Cal. Chart.* VI, 107.
26   *Cal. Chart.* I, 453.
27   *Cal. Pat.* 1211–72, 311.
28   Baigent & Millard, *Basingstoke*, 77, 316, 339.
29   *Cal. Chart.* V, 336.

Figure 7 *The agreement to go for arbitration with Sir John Wallop (1465) showing the seals of some of Basingstoke's citizens, here acting together.*

and subsequently it periodically appears in the documentation as a first floor hall and usually in relation to building decay.[30] Repairs were planned in 1570.[31] Later in 1656 the town hall was burnt down, but its successor, built in 1657, survived until the 19th century.[32] Like many towns, Basingstoke gained a charter of incorporation in the early 17th century (in 1622). From 1392 the governing body was restricted to 16 people, from whom two were to be elected each year as bailiffs,[33] but in many ways this merely formalised arrangements that already existed. The townsmen had already long been in control of their own affairs, and could act together in pursuit of the town's interest (Fig. 7).

The town was effectively administered through two types of court.[34] The regular three week courts or hundred courts dealt with matters of the concern to the smooth running of the town and community. It dealt with disputes about debts and trespasses, arguments and assaults; it made regulations for the community, such as those concerning the blocking of roads or ditches, and sometimes agreements about property or disputes are recorded. The courts provide long lists of disputes about debts. They tend to focus on who was involved, and the amount of the fines imposed by the court, rather than the cause, nature and size of the dispute or where the disputants came from, but they remind us of the importance of borrowing and debt for the smooth running of the economy. In addition, twice a year the court was held together with a view of frankpledge. These courts also involved representatives of the villages within the hundred as well as the town. The villages presented any serious offences that had taken place, any male who had not already been enrolled into the tithing, and any breaking of the trading regulations.

30   Baigent & Millard, *Basingstoke*, 82.
31   Baigent & Millard, *Basingstoke*, 347.
32   Baigent & Millard, *Basingstoke*, 62–3.
33   Baigent & Millard, *Basingstoke*, 439–52.
34   Based on court rolls and estreat rolls, HRO, 148M71/ 2/1 and 71/2/7 and selections published in Baigent & Millard, *Basingstoke*, 221–356.

The latter was restricted in the villages to fines on brewers and millers, but in the town this had been expanded in the 15th and 16th centuries to a wide range of occupations and these provide us with the list of occupations used in later chapters.[35]

The work of the courts was aided by several elected officials of the town. At the top were the two bailiffs. These were drawn from the wealthy of the town, and, particularly in the 16th century, from the dominant cloth industry, as well as occasional recruits from the local gentry (below, pp. 61–2). There were also under-bailiffs and constables with responsibility for maintaining the law. Agriculture was looked after by the common hayward, swineherd and a mower or keeper of the meadows.[36] Also elected were the assessors. In 1443, there was a steward.[37] In the 16th century, this post came to be held by the neighbouring, local lords, the Paulets of Basing, but for them it was an honorary post and so the post of deputy steward had to be created to fulfil the steward's responsibilities.

35   See also appendix, below.
36   e.g. Baigent & Millard, *Basingstoke*, 214, 234.
37   Baigent & Millard, *Basingstoke*, 273.

MEDIEVAL TOWNS MAY be defined by their economic role. They were places, however small, where a significant portion of the population relied on non-agricultural activities. They provided markets that linked the town with the country beyond, whether the villages immediately around, or those of distant ports and national imports and exports. Such markets depended on debts and good will, but the latter was not always found.

The court records of Basingstoke from the 15th and 16th centuries provide a great deal of information about the town's economic activity. There are cases of antisocial offences that incidentally shed light on agricultural or industrial pursuits. There are long list of those fined for pursuing particular occupations. These allow us both to see the wide range of occupations in the town and the dominant role of the cloth industry (see Figs 8 and 9). Although occasionally a detailed offence is recorded, these lists seem to represent a tax on specific occupations. The names and numbers for each occupation fluctuate, as one would expect, but individual names recur regularly in particular occupations over a prolonged period, and totals show discernible trends. They oversimplify the occupational structure since they do not take into account those who were engaged in more than one activity, but contemporaries would have recognised the main activities of their fellow citizens. The records are also full of the names of those involved in cases of debts. The courts covered small debts, with larger debts being dealt with by the royal courts, but these records are frustrating in their brevity. They do not usually tell us how much was involved and, when this has been stated, they seem small even by comparison with other small towns.[1] Occasionally, but not regularly, they tell us where one of those involved came from, usually from one of the neighbouring villages. Nor do they tell us what had caused the debt: was it for food or consumer goods? But frustrating as are such entries, they remind us of the economic reality of urban life.

Agriculture and the Town

Like other medieval towns, Basingstoke was surrounded by fields. It was both a producer of grain and meat and a consumer from its own fields and those of the villages around. The earliest map of Basingstoke is from 1762 (Maps 4 & 5) and gives an impression of the agriculture before inclosure of the open fields. Much of this pattern is medieval in origin and this is reinforced by earlier documentation from the 14th to 16th centuries. Agriculture was carried out in a series of great fenced fields which were subdivided into narrow strips. Basingstoke itself possessed four large open fields: to the north of the town was Chapel Field (formerly Northfield or Holy Ghost Field) and Salisbury Field

---

1   C. Dyer, 'Small towns, 1270–1540', *CUHB*, 524.

Figure 8 *Estreat roll of (1499) showing the start of the entries listing occupational fines.*

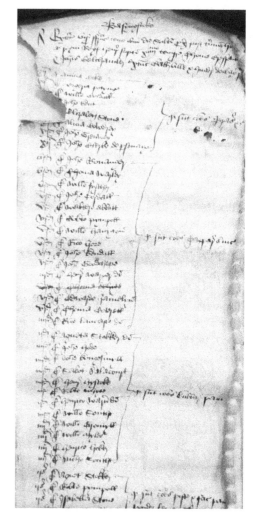

Figure 9 *Occupations fined: 1464–1535 (1638 entries). Source: see appendix. Building includes carpenters. Fullers included under cloth manufacture, although many would be appropriately described as mercantile.*

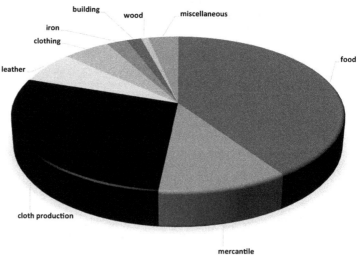

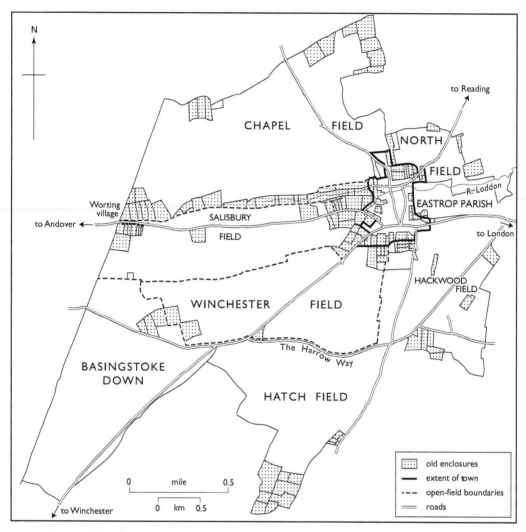

Map 4 *The open fields of Basingstoke: a reconstruction based on a map prepared for the Duke of Bolton in 1762.*

(or Westfield). To the south lay Winchester Field (probably Middelfield) and Hatch Field bounding the manor and parish of Hatch, which became a detached portion of Cliddesden in the late 14th century. East of the town and probably originally serving the small neighbouring settlement of Eastrop were Northfield (Northdown) and Hackfield (Map 4).[2] In addition to these open fields there were also common meadow lands such as Wildmore, providing hay and grass for animal feed, while the link between sheep and meadowland was also reflected in the name of one part of the meadows, 'sheep wash meadow'. There were also common downland pastures, particularly Basingstoke Down, to the south-west.[3] It is likely that such common lands had been encroached upon in the course of the Middle Ages, both resulting from the general population growth of the

2   Baigent & Millard, *Basingstoke*, 192–9, 617–22, 204–12, 622–30.
3   Baigent & Millard, *Basingstoke*, 283–4; Basingstoke Heath, alias sheepdown, 291.

Map 5 *Salisbury Field, one of the town's open fields: a map prepared for the Duke of Bolton in 1762.*

12th and 13th centuries, and of the growth of Basingstoke itself. The tenants possessed rights of pasture over the arable land, subject to local regulations.[4] However, other men did not possess such rights, such as John Fenkelen who pastured 20 pigs in the common of Ywolde, although he had no rights to do this.[5] There were woodlands, from Domesday Book onwards.[6]

The open fields were fenced around the outside in order to keep out animals from the growing crops. Inside, batches of strips would be divided by unploughed or grassy boundaries which had to be maintained despite periodic expansionist attempts to plough and control some of the land by neighbouring tenants.[7] Inclosure of land within the open field was forbidden and there are occasional examples of such offences being committed.[8] The open nature of the fields meant that agriculture had to be organised in a common, co-operative fashion for all the tenants. Arable land also served as common pasture for the tenants, although pasturing had to wait until after the harvest had been fully collected, when land would be left fallow in order to allow the soil the opportunity to rest and recover. This had to be a common policy and offenders were presented to the court.[9] The need for common regulations generated both disputes and documentation, as matters were presented to the view of frankpledge and to the manorial court. Ultimately conflict could be dealt with by these courts, but there were also local officials with oversight, above all the Hayward who was required to maintain the regulations. Thus in the view of Frankpledge in 1514, the jurors presented that various pigs had damaged the corn and the meadows 'but we cannot tell whose hogs they be, but the Hayward can'.[10]

Common field agriculture required cooperation by the tenants. Animals had to be kept off until the whole field had been harvested and removed. Loose animals could damage grain crops, as well as hay,[11] whether during the growing season or during harvest. After the grain had been removed, the field would be open to women and children to collect the remnants of the harvest. Only then could the animals take over and during the fallow period the fields would be used by the tenants' livestock. The latter, needed to be controlled to avoid overstocking. This was probably a particular worry with sheep, whether these were the possessions of tenants who exceeded their quotas or of neighbouring landowners or tenants who brought a flock from their lands to those of Basingstoke. Restrictions on the number of sheep was a common feature of the medieval centuries and after.[12] Moreover, sheep farming, especially for wool, but also for meat and milk, was a particular feature of the downland soils of the area. The Wallops, lords of neighbouring Farleigh seem to have been frequent offenders through overstocking, but other offenders included John Stocker of Eastrop, Richard Clerk the lessee of Eastrop, Richard Smith of Cliddesden or Richard Whithead, the lord of Eastrop.[13] Occasionally, the number of sheep are documented and this reflects the regional emphasis on large-

4   Baigent & Millard, *Basingstoke*, 298–300.
5   Baigent & Millard, *Basingstoke*, 272.
6   *Domesday*, 93.
7   Baigent & Millard, *Basingstoke*, 257, 99.
8   Baigent & Millard, *Basingstoke*, 334, 40.
9   Baigent & Millard, *Basingstoke*, 258, 384.
10   Baigent & Millard, *Basingstoke*, 317.
11   Baigent & Millard, *Basingstoke*, 227.
12   *Cal. Pat.* 1258–66, 680; Baigent & Millard, *Basingstoke*; HRO, 23M72/P1/2.
13   Baigent & Millard, *Basingstoke*, 273, 91, 99, 311, 348.

scale sheep farming in the later Middle Ages. John Wallop, the lord of Farleigh Wallop, was accused of trespassing with a flock of 700 sheep for almost a week in 1461, and Richard Smith of Cliddesden trespassed with 500 sheep in 1506.[14] Some of the infringements might have been due to outsiders crossing unclear lines of demarcation, but this was not always the case, as in 1583 when Richard Whithead's flock trespassed both to the nearby Hackwood Field and to the much further Holy Ghost Field.[15] Other flocks were on a smaller scale. In 1426 William Lowker folded 60 sheep in the South Field of Basingstoke, while in 1436 John Cowdray broke the rules by having 16 ewes belonging to outsiders in his fold, and in 1464–5 Thomas Kevesdale was fined for having 60 sheep in the field.[16] The large scale of the problem seems to have been particularly noticeable in the early 16th century, probably reflecting the boom conditions of the cloth industry. In 1535, tenants were allowed a stint of two sheep per acre of arable, and not more than five sheep for 2 a. of field land on the common called the Downe (Basingstoke Down, to the south-west beyond the open fields). The scale of the problem was reflected in the large fine of 20s for each offence.[17] Later in 1540, two leading figures in the town were asked to make a survey of the sheep on the manor in winter, and it was ordered that no one should keep more sheep in summer than in winter under penalty of 40s.[18]

Other livestock get specific mention in the court. Pigs are highlighted as they would damage the crops.[19] Another offence was catching rabbits on the arable land or from the warren.[20] The offenders may have been outsiders. One reference shows the presence of a common rabbit catcher on the common, whose offence was to catch rabbits from a neighbouring lordship.[21] Occasionally the offender was specified as the keeper of one of the neighbouring gentry parks at Hackwood or Privett.[22] Such practices were probably longstanding but poorly documented. Domesday, for example, hints at the opportunities for such mixed farming in the 11th century without providing an overall picture. There was land for 20 ploughs, including three for the lord and eight for the smallholders and four for the freemen. Pastoral farming was represented by 20 a. of meadow and woodland for 20 pigs.[23]

The sub-manor belonging to the hospital of St John, provides us with intermittent, varied and limited documentation for the later 13th and early 14th centuries.[24] The hospital was involved in direct cultivation of both grain and livestock. The accounts record the labour costs of ploughing, carting, mowing the meadows, weeding, harvesting, threshing and winnowing. The main crops were wheat, maslin (a wheat-rye mix), barley and oats. The domination of wheat mixes and oats was typical of the sowing practices of this area reflecting the poor quality of the soils. Power was largely

14   Baigent & Millard, *Basingstoke*, 291, 311. The Wallop dispute may eventually have been dealt with by arbitration, see 298–303.
15   Baigent & Millard, *Basingstoke*, 348.
16   Baigent & Millard, *Basingstoke*, 259, 265, 296.
17   Baigent & Millard, *Basingstoke*, 325.
18   Baigent & Millard, *Basingstoke*, 331.
19   Baigent & Millard, *Basingstoke*, 273, 287, 317, 324.
20   Baigent & Millard, *Basingstoke*, 271, 275, 282, 303, 307, 308.
21   Baigent & Millard, *Basingstoke*, 308.
22   Baigent & Millard, *Basingstoke*, 303.
23   *Domesday*, 93.
24   Based on Merton Coll., 4333, 41, 42, 46, 56, 50; Baigent & Millard, *Basingstoke*, 630–7.

provided by horses, as in 1401–3.[25] The estate had a cattle breeding herd and produced butter and cheeses. There was also a herd of pigs ranging in size, from about 10 to over 20.[26] The farm seemed to have increased the range of livestock by 1333, when there was a substantial flock of over 100 sheep.[27] Earlier than this, the sheep numbers were not recorded, although the presence is made clear by the cost of the shepherd moving the sheep fold. It is not clear when the hospital gave up direct cultivation and leased the farm out to a tenant, since the documentation is missing for the period 1347–66, but the manor was leased out by the latter date.[28]

Cloth Industry

Like most medieval towns, Basingstoke produced cloth for a local market, although little direct evidence survives. In the 13th century, the town had been a focus of the trade in wool. It then became part of the transformation of England from an exporter of wool to one of cloth that took place in the later Middle Ages. Nationally cloth exports had already dramatically increased sixfold in the 14th century, but they continued to grow. The 15th century saw a slowdown and a recession in mid century but recovered and still increased by 50 per cent in the century as a whole and continued to expand sharply until the mid 16th century.[29] Hampshire was part of this national growth, particularly in the east of the county in the areas around Basingstoke and Alton. In the 14th century, the West Country, above all Somerset and Wiltshire, had been the great growth area for cloth production. In the following centuries, this extended eastwards to north-east Hampshire and the Thames Valley. The latter was an area that, like Basingstoke, produced the lighter smaller kersies rather than the traditional full broadcloth, catering for the demand for middle range cloths both in England and on the continent. Its cloth was exported through London and Southampton, since in the 15th century the latter was the most active exporter of cloth outside London. There are occasional references in the Southampton brokage books (which recorded the port's inland trade) to Basingstoke cloth, although these books do not usually list cloth brought into the port. In 1528, consignments of over 200 cloths were exported from Basingstoke through Southampton. But the town was also within the orbit of London which was the pre-eminent cloth exporting port of the period. More than anything else, it was the growth of the cloth industry that helped to transform the town, and allowed Basingstoke to reach its position of national prominence by 1524/5.[30] (See Fig. 10 and appendix.)

25   Merton Coll., 4341, 4342.
26   Merton Coll., 4341–2, 50.
27   Merton Coll., 4350.
28   Merton Coll., 4356; Baigent & Millard, *Basingstoke*, 640. Its continued leasing is seen in H.E. Salter (ed.), *Registrum annalium collegii Mertoniensis: 1483–1521* (Oxford Hist. Soc., 1923), 85, 112, 132, 138, 268; J.M. Fletcher (ed.), *1521–67* (Oxford Hist. Soc., 1974), passim.
29   For national figures see E.M. Carus-Wilson and O. Coleman, *England's Export Trade, 1275–1547* (1963).
30   See above, 5–6; A. Dyer, 'Ranking lists of English medieval towns', *CUHB*, 755–67.

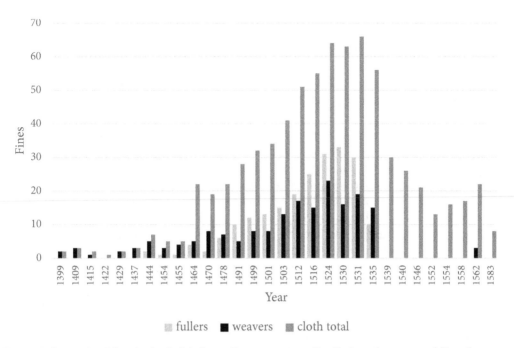

Figure 10 *Occupational fines in the cloth industry. Source: see appendix. Cloth total = weavers, fullers, dyer, mercers, drapers, clothiers. The system of fines was altered between 1535 and 1539, hence the drop in numbers.*

There was only limited production in the town at the start of the 15th century, as seen in the aulnage accounts which record the receipts from a tax on cloth sales.[31] In 1394/5, at a time of considerable growth of cloth production elsewhere in the country, Basingstoke, unlike the small Hampshire towns of Alton, Alresford and Andover, did not warrant its own specific entry in these accounts.[32] Things were beginning to change by 1402, when Basingstoke and Alton, the future major cloth producing centres in Hampshire, had their own entry and together listed seven names, but the evidence for expansion in the early part of the century is limited.[33] By 1467, this had changed further, and the town and nearby Odiham had become important centres registering 4.8 per cent of the county's cloth, although the town still remained substantially less important than Winchester, Romsey, and Alton and its neighbours.[34] But Basingstoke's industrial growth continued at a greater rate in the later 15th and early 16th centuries as shown by the fines for breaking the assize, which were in effect payments for pursuing particular occupations within the town: a business tax to provide cash for the town's expenses. The

31 Criticism of the reliability of the aulnage accounts was made by E.M. Carus-Wilson, who showed that some of the later accounts were fabrications, *Medieval Merchant Venturers* (1954), 279–91. Continued use has shown that the accounts criticised were not typical and that the source deserves further but cautious use: J. Hare, 'Growth and recession in the fifteenth-century economy: the Wiltshire textile industry and the countryside', *Econ. Hist. Rev.* 52 (1999), 2.

32 Keene, *Medieval Winchester*, 316; Hare, 'Regional prosperity in fifteenth-century England: some evidence from Wessex', 115.

33 TNA, E 101/344/17 m. 1.

34 TNA, E 101/344/17 m. 18.

records should be treated with caution and periodically the townsmen seem to have reassessed the criteria, so that weavers and fullers disappeared from the fines between 1535 and 1541. Nevertheless, they provide us with an important source for evaluating the trends in the cloth industry. In 1399, there were only two weavers and no others recorded as engaged in this industry. There was some growth by the 1440s, followed by a fall in the 1450s, probably associated with the general recession in England during these years. There then followed a period of growth gathering momentum as the century progressed. The number of townsmen fined for involvement in cloth production or marketing rose:[35] from five in 1454 to 19 in 1474. After a period of stability this increased, particularly after 1485: 28 in 1491, 41 in 1503, 55 in 1516 and 67 in 1524, then stabilising to 66 in 1531 (Fig. 10). Basingstoke was part of later waves of national expansion, in the early 15th century and above all in the late 15th and early 16th centuries. The cloth industry was clearly booming by the early 16th century. Within this broad chronology, the periods of greatest growth seem to have been the 1460s, and from *c.*1490–*c.*1530. The changing figure thereafter, with its dramatic fall probably resulted from a change in the system of occupational fines, rather than from any dramatic economic decline. This change was particularly noticeable in 1535–9, when the fines ceased to include weavers and fullers.

The growth of this industry saw the emergence of large-scale cloth entrepreneurs. This was already evident in 1467 when Nicholas Draper, also known as Nicholas Bayly, marketed 160 kersies, or nearly 60 per cent of the cloth from Basingstoke and Odiham.[36] He was a noted cloth trader. He is first seen fined as a tailor in 1444, but was then the first to be fined as a draper from 1447 to 1470, described as a draper in 1468, and then fined as a mercer in 1470. He was actively involved as a major player in town life being bailiff in 1465–6, leasing the rectory in 1470–1, and he acted both as a feoffee in land transactions and as a representative of the town. He provides an early example of the increasing role of the cloth men in the running of the town and its economy.[37] Another early cloth entrepreneur was Henry Horne, who was a draper from 1461–70, and John Horne who was the second most important figure in the aulnage account for 1467.[38]

The raw wool was first washed and then spun, although much of this may have been done in the countryside. Wool would have come from the great sheep flocks on the downland around, although increasingly wool was probably drawn from further afield. The wool that came in tithes to the vicar in the early 16th century was sold to local cloth traders, such as to Thomas South, John and Thomas Kyngesmill.[39] Spinning was probably performed by hand although spinning wheels were increasingly used in the 16th century as reflected in later inventories. Most of this would have been done by women and since this was a supplementary occupation, we know very little of their activities. They seem to be a blank in the documentation. Spinners, for example, are never included in the occupational fines. Once the wool was spun it was woven into various forms of cloth. The traditional heavy broad cloth was much more common in the older centres such as Winchester and Andover, but not in Basingstoke. In the 15th century it was the smaller

35   Production: weavers, fullers, dyer; marketing: mercers, drapers, clothiers. The categories overlap.
36   TNA, E 101/344/17 m. 18 (the account does not separate the traders between Basingstoke and Odiham); Himsworth, *Winchester Coll.* II, 186.
37   Himsworth, *Winchester Coll.* II, 183; HRO, 148M71/2/1/52; 2/7/3; 2/7/7; Macray, *Selborne*, 22.
38   TNA, E 101/344/17 m. 18; HRO, 148M71; 2/1/63; 2/7/7; Himsworth, *Winchester Coll.* II 183.
39   C.U.L., MS Ll.2.2., 3r.

mid-weight kersies that were increasingly important and this lay at the heart of the industry of the town and its hinterland, as well as that of Alton, as shown in the aulnage accounts.[40]

After weaving, the cloth had to be finished by a succession of processes. The first of these, fulling, involved soaking the cloth in a solution of urine and fuller's earth, to clean and shrink it, followed by stretching it on racks or tenters, raising the nap with teasels and then shearing this off. The object of these processes was to provide a much smoother surface to the cloth. The final stage involved the shearing of the surface and the repair of any knots or defects. Increasingly the industry used heavy water-powered beating of the cloth rather than the more gentle foot fulling (trampling the cloth in the solution) so characteristic of earlier urban production. The town became surrounded by a series of fulling mills, around which gathered the rural spinners and weavers (see below). Increasingly the term 'fuller' was used as a term to denote traders and finishers of the cloth, often trading on a large scale.

The wool or cloth also had to be coloured either by dyeing the wool before weaving[41] or dyeing the cloth itself. This was done in a variety of colours either using English or imported natural dyestuffs such as woad or madder or the mordant (fixative) alum, and brought from Southampton or London. Dyeing colours recorded in the inventories included black, grey, sky, horse flesh, mackerel, lavender, yellow, primrose, French green, sad green, holly green, sea green, blue, purple and red.[42] Since both fulling and dyeing required water, both processes would have been found in the northern lower part of the town by the river. The liquid refuse of the dyeing process was dumped in the river, and therefore needed to be regulated and restricted to anti-social hours. Emptying the dyeing vats was therefore forbidden during the day.[43]

Much of the cloth was produced in the countryside and then marketed in the town. Production in the countryside increasingly focussed on a growing group of rural fulling mills, but was also linked to the neighbouring satellite towns of Odiham and Overton. Basingstoke's role was a mixture of production, finishing and marketing. This included finishing and final quality control of local products. The town authorities could also regulate the cloth.[44] Some cloth came from much further afield. Thus in 1583, William Crome (woollen draper) owed money to Thomas Harryson (Kendalman) presumably for the purchase of cloth. Kendalmen, from the Lake District in the far north-west of England, were also regular visitors to Southampton in the early 16th century.[45] By the late 16th century, some of the cloth produced and sold in the area, was in the form of bays or frises, some of the new draperies: smaller, lighter and cheaper cloths using combed rather than the carded wool. Something of the variety of cloth can be seen in the inventory of William Crome, woollen draper, in 1583. His shop contained, amongst others, broad northern black, Dorsetshire white, Flanders dyed kerseys, Western black kersey, broad bays in black, green, blue and ash colour, and narrow purple bays, red frysadoe (frises), grey and black fryse and red, black, white and green cotton.[46]

40   TNA, E 101/344/17 m. 18.
41   e.g. HRO, 1570B/1/56.
42   HRO, 1581B/111; 1570B/1/56; 1583B/23, 1587/B/82; 1606B2/2.
43   As in 1505 between 3 a.m. and 9 p.m. or in 1556 between 6 a.m. and 6 p.m. (Baigent & Millard, *Basingstoke*, 310, 343).
44   Baigent & Millard, *Basingstoke*, 275.
45   J. Hare, 'Southampton's trading partners: beyond Hampshire and Wiltshire', *English Inland Trade*, 110.
46   HRO, 1583/B/23.

The cloth industry within the town was at its peak in the 1520s. Fortunately, this was at the very time when the 1523 tax assessment was particularly full, and so we can then correlate the listing of occupational fines with the taxable wealth. Here a threefold assessment by wealth has been adopted: the rich who paid £1 or more in the tax, the poor who paid the minimum 4*d.*, and the middling sort who paid amounts in between (mostly from 1*s.* 6*d.* to 5*s.*) (see below, pp. 58–61).[47] At least 28 per cent of those assessed in the 1523 subsidy were also fined for infringement of the assize and can be given an occupation. Almost half (at least 42 per cent) of those who were fined were involved in cloth production and marketing, emphasising the importance of the industry.

The cloth industry dominated the rich of the town and its political elite. Of the 18, amongst the rich, whose occupation can be established, twelve were in the cloth industry (three mercers, two drapers and seven fullers), and the rest were innkeepers, in the leather industry and a butcher. The cloth trade occupied at least about two thirds of this financial elite. Wealth and cloth also brought power in the local community. About half of this group also appeared on the incomplete list of bailiffs, the main official who ran the town. Of the known bailiffs between 1510 and 1539, 65 per cent were fullers and mercers, a marked contrast to the situation in the early 15th century (see below, Table 3).[48]

Amongst the richest were the mercers, who engaged in the import of luxury textile and a variety of consumer goods as well as trading in cloth. In the assessments for the 1523 subsidy, the three mercers, Richard Ronanger, Robert Pether and Thomas Lane, were assessed between £2 and £3.[49] An indication of the range of their activities can be seen by examining the inventory of Thomas Lane who died in 1532.[50] The possessions in his inventory included various types of linen, shirts, hats, sewing thread, sewing silks, drugs, oils and spices, figs and currents, paper and books, although there does not seem to have then been ordinary cloth in store. He also possessed links to other leading figures in the town like Belchamber and Canner (see below, pp. 60, 70, 42). Meanwhile, a mercer, from a slightly earlier period who had recently died but showed many of these same features was John Boyer who flourished from 1490 to 1514, acting as mercer and fishmonger from 1491 to 1503, chandler and draper in 1491, bailiff in 1491, 1511, 1514, and who leased the rectory in 1490–8 when described as a merchant.[51]

The rich also included, two of the five drapers, although none were among the very richest, and one draper at 5*s.* fell into our middling category. Of the two amongst the rich, Hugh Lancaster was fined from 1516 to 1524 and was able to apprentice two sons to a London merchant; and John Hoskyns, was fined as a draper from 1512 to 1524.[52]

Fullers finished the cloth giving it the required surface texture, soaking and cleaning the cloth, shrinking and stretching it, and raising the nap and trimming, but they also evidently acquired a much wider trading role, and showed an extremely wide range of wealth. They grew substantially in numbers from 1478 and particularly from 1491 (10) to 1531 (30). Some were evidently craftsmen and practicing fullers with the minimal payment of 4*d.* in 1523, but others were among the richest men in the town, who had

47   HRO, 148M71/3/4/2.
48   Listed in Baigent & Millard, *Basingstoke*, 434–7. Occupations from fines (see appendix).
49   HRO, 148M71/2/7/17–20.
50   HRO, 1532B/09.
51   HRO, 148M71/33/4/2; 2/7/9, 2/7/14, 2/7/16; Baigent & Millard, *Basingstoke*, 436; Mag. Coll., 5615.
52   HRO, 148M71/2/7/17; 2/7/18–22.

evidently become large-scale entrepreneurs and were amongst the dominant figures in the cloth trade. Of the 27 fullers who we can comment on, ten paid the minimum assessment, eleven paid in the mid-range and six were among the richest of the town. Of the five highest payments three were for fullers. Robert Stocker was amongst these, three times bailiff, a fuller in 1516 and 1524, and he also brewed.[53] The Stocker family continued as cloth merchants (see below, pp. 63–4). Another rich fuller, William Locker was also a mercer and fishmonger in 1530 and 1531 while a predecessor had earlier been a mercer in 1491.[54] The Kingsmill family had been well-established in the town throughout the 15th century, with Richard a particularly wealthy and influential figure in the town beyond the fulling trade (see below, pp. 67–9). The fulling branch may be seen in the industry from mid century, albeit not amongst the wealthiest of the townsmen. William was one of the two first fullers to be fined in 1443, and continued fulling until at least 1470.[55] John Kingsmill fuller (or a father and son) was bailiff, four times between 1503 and 1510, and built a new fulling mill in the countryside. In 1524, a Richard Kingsmill was a fuller, and another member of the family was a miller, although with a much smaller assessment.[56]

In contrast to the fullers, most weavers were probably small-scale independent producers, with twelve out of the eighteen assessed at the minimum level. The other six were in the mid-range, although mainly in the middle of this group. Such men were probably engaged in trading in others' cloth on a small scale but unlike some of the fullers they were not among the great entrepreneurs.

Occupational fines for clothiers do not begin until the 1530s. This coincides with the apparent disappearance of fullers from the occupational fines, and suggests a recognition of the long-term shift of the fullers from craftsmen, who finished the cloth, to traders in cloth. This entrepreneurial role was already evident by the enormous wealth of some of the fullers in the 1523 tax assessments. Some of the clothiers would have also taken responsibility for the fulling of the cloth, although increasingly the latter stage was focussed on water mills in the countryside around (below, p. 53). Others also possessed looms and other production equipment.[57] Initially drapers were still fined separately from clothiers.

Dyers were few in numbers and with a much smaller range of assessments. In 1523, two paid the minimum assessment two were in the mid-range. They may have been engaged in trading, but they were essentially craftsmen and small-scale entrepreneurs. William Gilbert was fined as a dyer from 1524 to 1544, with a mid-range tax payment in 1523.[58] Subsequently in 1544, his successor, Roger Gilberd, left an inventory showing a household that contained the necessary equipment for dyeing. In the wool house was a kersey, wool, yarn and supplies of alum and madder for dyeing. His debts included £4–10s. to a Londoner, probably for such dyestuffs, and the money he was owed included that from two men for whom he had dyed cloths known as watchets, after the town on the west Somerset coast.[59]

53   Hare, 'Southampton's trading partners: the small towns of Hampshire and Wiltshire', *English Inland Trade*, 97; on the family see below, 63–4.
54   HRO, 148M71/2/7/9, 2/7/18-22.
55   HRO, 148M71/2/1/46; 2/7/7.
56   HRO, 148M71/2/7/18; Baigent & Millard, *Basingstoke*, 436.
57   HRO, 1581AD/17.
58   HRO, 148M71/2/7/18, 2/7/24.
59   HRO, 21M65/D3/40.

Even though occupational fines make it clear that the town was a manufacturing centre for cloth, it was even more important as a centre for trading and finishing. In 1524, there was a substantial group of weavers (23) but many more than this were engaged in trading or finishing cloth, three mercers and five drapers, 28 fullers and five dyers, when each of these occupations would have needed to be supported by many weavers. This implies that the town, while producing cloth, must have been heavily dependent on the production of the villages around and this is reinforced by the evidence from the villages themselves (see below, pp. 51–6). The structure of the urban cloth industry was both complex and varied. Some of those fined were self-employed craftsmen who wove the cloth, although much of this would have been made in the villages nearby. Clothiers operated on a larger scale; they employed labour and would have taken part in manufactures as well as buying cloth from individual craftsmen.[60] In addition, specialist tasks could be performed at commission as in dyeing and fulling. Such craftsmen might work on their own account so that occasionally we find undyed wool at the dyehouse, among the dyed wools and cloths.[61] Cloth could be fulled externally on commission at a fulling mill.[62] Clothiers might also employ labour on production as represented by the presence in individual inventories of spinning wheels[63] and looms,[64] or by putting out work outside their house and workshop, whether paying weavers in the town or supplying a loom on loan.[65] The inventories of the 'shops', or workshops, might record the presence of cloths, but a standard feature was the provision for finishing the cloth: the boards and shears.[66] Other inventories show evidence of fulling in the racks and teasels. Different industrial elements could be brought together, but equally broken apart. When clothier, John West, the younger, died in 1596 he split his business among his children: one received his narrow fulling racks, another was to have the dyehouse, the third his broad looms, and the last his fuller's shop for broad cloth.[67]

The continuing importance of the cloth industry in the 16th century is reflected in the occupational fines, in the inventories of the town's clothiers, and in the Southampton brokage books. It is difficult to be precise on the town's fortunes, but they probably reflected the national trends in cloth exports, with growth until mid century followed by a period of difficulty and uncertainty. Although the number of fines declined sharply from 66 in 1531 to 30 in 1540, this seems to represent a change in the system of fines rather than of economic decline. The two largest groups, the fullers and weavers, were no longer being included, although the former were probably now described as clothiers. In 1540, 42 carts were sent to Basingstoke from Southampton, much more than the ten and under in the 15th century, or even the 22 carts in 1528.[68]

60   TNA, PROB 11/88/350.
61   HRO, 1570B/156.
62   HRO, 1571B/193.
63   HRO, 1574B/136; 1571B/193; 1588AD/48.
64   HRO, 1563A/15, 1573AD 32, 1574B/177; 1596AD/81.
65   TNA, PROB 11/88/350; HRO, 1574B/177.
66   HRO, 1557U/230; 1574B/136; 1576AD/52; 1581AD/17; 21M65/D2/13.
67   TNA, PROB 11/88/350.
68   Hare, 'Southampton's trading partners: the small towns of Hampshire and Wiltshire', *English Inland Trade*, 97.

In the second half of the century, at a time when our evidence shifts in nature, it becomes more difficult to establish the long-term trends from specific Basingstoke evidence. The tax assessments become much more restricted and less valuable, while the occupational fines in this industry are restricted to drapers, dyers and mercers or merchants. Nevertheless, changes occurred: Southampton's cloth exports, and particularly its exports of Hampshire kersies, on which Basingstoke's prosperity had been based, collapsed between 1565 and 1588/9. This was, however, less disastrous than might have appeared since most Hampshire kersies, were now exported through London, seven times as much as through Southampton in 1565/6. Nevertheless, the difficulties of the London trade would have affected Basingstoke and Hampshire. For slightly under half the year in 1565, 22,226 Hampshire kersies had been exported through London and Southampton, but for the whole year of 1619 this had fallen to 6,854.[69] The industry remained important as shown in the inventories of its traders, as did the town itself, although the town probably now lost out in relative terms to Romsey, Christchurch and Ringwood.[70]

Feeding the Town

Like other towns, Basingstoke produced some of its food in the fields that surrounded it, but the essence of a town was that it possessed a large number of people who were engaged in full time crafts and who needed to be fed. The town was largely dependent for its food on its hinterland. The growth of the cloth industry here, would have generated a wide range of occupations both those working within the industry and among those who served the cloth workers and traders. All of these would need to be fed, and the town would be a major centre of food consumption. In some cases, food was brought from a distance particularly with wine and fish, as documented in the trade from Southampton (below, pp. 47–9). Entrepreneurs brought the goods from the port into the town from where it was distributed through smaller-scale traders. Other products came from the immediate agricultural hinterland, particularly grain, meat and other products of pastoral farming. Here, as in other urban centres, the governing groups showed a concern to maintain the free market and to prevent forestalling and regrating, which involved buying up particular goods to create monopolies, and thus pushed up the price to the consumer. Occasionally, there were examples of blatant fraud. In 1520 one presentment was of Richard Hoore, 'who doth buy by one bushel and selleth with another' thus enhancing his profits and inflating the price of the grain.[71]

The occupational fines demonstrate the importance of the food industries in production and marketing. Each year about 50 people were fined for pursuing activities in the food trade from brewers and tavern-keepers, to butchers, bakers and fishmongers, numbers that reflect a thoroughly urban context. Interestingly despite the growing size of the town, and despite minor annual fluctuations in particular occupations, the number remained at about this level throughout the period until the later drop in numbers in

69   Rosen, 'Winchester in transition', 149.
70   Rosen, 'Winchester in transition', 175.
71   Baigent & Millard, *Basingstoke*, 324.

1546 (see appendix). Some of the highest fines were for inns, fishmongers and bakers, perhaps in attempt to tax those holding monopolies or controls over essentials.

Brewers and Tapsters

The falling numbers involved in brewing and selling reflected the shift from ale to beer. The use of hops produced a drink with a longer life span and thus allowed larger-scale production, and a shift from small-scale production and sale by the alewife. This was one of the key developments of the period 1450–1550 in the South East, spreading from London, and from town to countryside.[72] The importation of hops through Southampton, and its growth, has been documented in the brokage books. Here only occasional references occur before the 1490s: only Salisbury and Winchester were destinations for hops in 1440–63. Beer appeared first in those places where large-scale production was most advantageous and concentrated. In the later and more frequent brokage accounts from the 16th century, Salisbury and Winchester still predominated, but hops were now also sent to the smaller towns: to Basingstoke as well as to Andover, Romsey and Hungerford.[73] It should be noted, however, that much of the hops would have come as unrecorded imports through London, where we have no comparable documentation. This would have been particularly the case in somewhere like Basingstoke, which was relatively close to the capital.

Brewing thus became less the product of household production by the sellers themselves and increasingly of a large-scale specialist manufacture for sale to small-scale sellers. Despite the growth of the town, the number of brewers fell rapidly. There was an early drop from 34 to 22 in 1422, but thereafter they remained steady until the major drop towards the end of the 15th century. They fell from 21 in 1478, to 11 in 1485, nine in 1524, and four in 1531. The evidence suggests that by 1524, the brewers were well entrenched within the middle range of wealth, with no one paying less than 2*s.* 6*d.* The two amongst the rich were wealthy cloth traders, Thomas Lane was a mercer and Henry Lee was a fuller, and they would have supported brewing as an additional source of investment and profit. But the growth of the town also meant the need for more drinking outlets. Meanwhile, in 1422 there were four tapsters, among the drink sellers, rising to 15 in 1437 with another sharp rise in level to 25 in 1485, broadly remaining at that level thereafter until 1531. They were generally much poorer than the brewers, even though the family might have used the role of alewife as a second income. It is noticeable that the vicar's sales of his malt tithes were generally specified by Gossmer as to women, in contrast to the partly male list of those fined as brewers or tapsters.[74] In 1523, ten of the sixteen people fined, paid at the basic level of assessment, and only six in the mid-range of assessments.

72   For the importance of the change, see M.E. Mate, *Trade and Economic Developments, 1450–1550: the Experience of Kent, Surrey, and Sussex* (2006), 60–80.
73   Hare, 'Miscellaneous goods', *English Inland Trade*, 161.
74   C.U.L., MS Ll.2.2, 4r.

Bakers and Grain Supply

There were generally two bakers fined annually in the period up to 1470, rising to six or seven in 1502–16. They were generally highly fined reflecting the role of bread as a basic necessity. As in 1427, there seems to have been a particular concern about the selling of underweight loaves.[75] It should be noted that urban production was probably supplemented by bread produced in the countryside around, as with that of William Stevens of Tadley in 1588.[76] The four town bakers in 1523, were all within the mid-range of assessments. The town regulators sought to fix the price of bread, and its size, with adequate numbers of small loaves.[77] Occasionally the inventories can provide a sense of the specialist baking shop that lay behind these activities, as with William Perman.[78]

Millers

Three mills were recorded in Domesday Book.[79] The occupational fines suggest a similar number in the early 15th century, varying from two to four. They peaked at five or six in 1491–1512. Given the capital required to set up a new mill, such growth is more interesting than an occasional vacant mill, and reflects a growing demand for flour. A new mill required capital investment albeit the new mills may have been on a small scale. Not all were water mills, and a horse-driven mill in Wote Street belonged to the Holy Ghost Guild.[80] The fluctuations in the number of millers may have reflected the use of the latter type of mill. The names of the two main mills are documented, Houndsmill and Kingsmill.[81] Of the two millers in 1524, one paid at the minimum rate, while the other, from a branch of the Kingsmill family, was amongst the middling sort. The miller's role provided the opportunity and dangers of dominating or monopolising the market and this was recognised in a decree forbidding millers buying grain in the market, either by themselves or through an agent.[82]

Fishmongers

Fish provided an important source of food, reinforced by the encouragement of the church. From the early 14th century it had become much more accessible, thanks to the development of the techniques of salt curing which enhanced the keeping qualities of sea fish, such as herring, allowing them to be preserved for over a year.[83] Herring were landed at the port in barrels, carried from there in this form, and then opened up and sold off in smaller quantities as appropriate. At the end of our period the fish traders were among the rich of the town and often engaged in the export of cloth. The

---

75 Baigent & Millard, *Basingstoke*, 260.
76 Baigent & Millard, *Basingstoke*, 335.
77 Baigent & Millard, *Basingstoke*, 314, 317, 320, 347.
78 HRO, 1588AD/48.
79 *Domesday*, 93.
80 Millard, *Holy Ghost*, 41; Himsworth, *Winchester Coll.* II, 189.
81 HRO, 148M71/2/1/10.
82 Baigent & Millard, *Basingstoke*, 339.
83 M. Kowaleski, 'The expansion of the south-western fisheries in late medieval England', *Econ. Hist. Rev.* 53 (2000), 429–54; J. Hare, 'Fish' in *English Inland Trade*, 147–51.

linkage of these two trades may seem surprising but made economic sense. Their sale of cloth in the ports would have left the merchants with money to reinvest and bring back in the form of fish which would then make a further profit. In 1524 there were two fishmongers, both rich mercers, Richard Ronanger and Thomas Lane. This linkage seems typical of the latter part of the period. Thus, in 1503, of the five fishmongers, four were mercers and one was a draper.[84] In 1491, there were two, both of whom were mercers. Richard Ronanger, a rich mercer, also incidentally sheds light on how the trade continued within the town, as in 1503 he (or his servant) sold fish from a board on the roadside to the annoyance of his neighbours. It was clearly a temporary stall and he was ordered to remove it at night.[85] The objection was to the location of the board not to what he was doing. The brokage books suggest that the fish trade had grown by 1540 and that it was increasingly dominated by a group of Southampton merchants.[86] Several entries in the town records suggest that innkeepers were monopolising the selling of fish and pushing up the price, with one regulation seeking to insist that innkeepers should not buy fish before the bailiffs had seen it openly on display.[87]

Butchers

There were usually three or four butchers who were fined, but occasionally this ranged more widely from one to seven (see appendix). In the 1520s two butchers were fined, one from among the rich and well-established of the town and one from the mid-range. William Grete, the wealthier of the two and who was evidently a man of importance in the town, was fined as a butcher between 1499 and 1523.[88] His importance in the community is reflected in his appointments as bailiff in 1530 and warden of the Holy Ghost guild in 1536. It should be emphasised that William Grete should be seen as a wholesale meat trader rather than as a small-scale shop keeper. The butchering and fish trade was probably reflected in John Grete's import of salt from Southampton in 1528.[89] The family diversified by the 1540s, with one William Grete becoming a draper in Basingstoke and another becoming a burgess of Southampton where he seems to have concentrated on the fish trade, particularly with Basingstoke, while a third left for education and ended up as vicar of nearby Heckfield.[90] The Grete family were known in the town from at least 1398, where they were already engaged in the butchering trade. Richard Grete was fined as a butcher (1392–1415) and had a shop in the market place.[91] Later, from 1422 to 1444, Thomas Grete and John Grete were both butchers and in 1427 they were accused of killing a bull without licence. In 1436, Thomas possessed 18 more pigs than he should have had according to the regulation, and both witnessed a legal

---

84 One John Boyer was both fishmonger and mercer in 1491 and 1503, leased the rectory in 1490 and 1497, was a bailiff in 1514 and was described as a merchant in 1490, Mag. Coll., EL/1 f79 (catalogue).
85 Baigent & Millard, *Basingstoke*, 310.
86 See below, 47–8.
87 Baigent & Millard, *Basingstoke*, 314, 334.
88 HRO, 148M71/2/7/12; 2/7/18.
89 *Overland Trade Database.*
90 Hare, 'Southampton's trading partners: the small towns of Hampshire and Wiltshire', *English Inland Trade*, 96. J. Foster, *Alumni Oxonienses, 1500–1714* (Oxford, 1891), 601.
91 Baigent & Millard, *Basingstoke*, 244, 248; HRO, 148M71/2/1/8.

dispute over land in 1443, and took part in assaults in 1449/50.[92] They were both fined as butchers in 1448, but by 1454 the business had passed to another generation, William and Hugh. William Grete, who was fined as a butcher between 1454 and 1478, was one of the townsmen involved in the new regulations or constitutions of 1465.[93] Such men traded in meat over a wide area, as reflected in the will of a later William Grete in 1540, who gave bequests to the parish church of Basingstoke and eleven surrounding villages.[94] His successor, with the same name, contributed to the fund for the restoration of the Holy Ghost chapel.[95] The surviving inventories can also shed light on the world of the butchers. Sometimes they kept substantial numbers of livestock of their own, as with John Lypescome in 1568 who possessed three 'hoggs', eighteen pigs and six cattle.[96] Another John Lippescome in 1575 possessed eight cattle, 83 sheep and 20 pigs.[97] We can also see John and William in action selling lambs for the dinner of the Fraternity of the Holy Ghost in 1559 and John also making a substantial contribution to the Fraternity in 1557.[98]

Cheese, Eggs and Miscellaneous Food Products

Our documentary evidence of medieval food, for Basingstoke as elsewhere, tends to concentrate on the basic foodstuffs: grain, meat, fish and drink. There were other goods in the town such as the luxuries, including the spices from the distant Mediterranean, found in Thomas Lane's shop.[99] There were also the other local foodstuffs that were required by households. A small, poor local monastic household of Cistercian nuns at Wintney Priory, 10 miles north-west of Basingstoke, could be seen as representative of the more affluent urban households, and required cheese, butter and eggs.[100] These, and local fruits and vegetables, would be usually produced and marketed in small quantities in the town, although the area would soon be seeing a growing emphasis on pastoral farming and cheese production. Occasionally, there would be references to trading activities when the market was seen as being abused by men buying up goods in order to push up the price, as with Robert Pytte in 1511 for butter, eggs and cheese, and Christopher Thacker and John Blauden in 1550 for eggs and cheese.[101]

Consumer Goods and Services

Towns were a point of interaction between the specialist manufactures, trades and services of the town and the countryside of its hinterland, with its food to supply and

---

92 HRO, 148M71/2/7/1–2/1/47; Baigent & Millard, *Basingstoke*, 261, 265, 270, 274, 280. Thomas had earlier been a carpenter (HRO, 148M71/2/1/15).

93 HRO, 148M71/2/7/4; Baigent & Millard, *Basingstoke*, 298, 301.

94 HRO, 1540B37: Basing, Cliddesden, Preston, Dummer, Oakley, Worting, Wotton, West Sherborne, Sherfield, Shirborne St John, Bramley.

95 Millard, *Holy Ghost*, 2.

96 HRO, 1540B/78/2.

97 HRO, 1575B/44.

98 Millard, *Holy Ghost*, 10, 2.

99 See below, 50.

100 Hare, 'The nuns of Wintney priory and their manor of Herriard', *PHFC* 70 (2015), 198–9.

101 Baigent & Millard, *Basingstoke*, 316, 339.

demands for what the town could offer. The presence of such urban specialism is often undocumented and speculative. By the 13th and 14th century Basingstoke had become one of the more important towns in the county and its provision of specialism is already reflected in occasional surnames in the 1327 tax assessments or other sources: a baker, a cooper, a wheeler, a tailor, a carpenter and a weaver.[102] There was a Potters Street by 1473, suggesting the presence of metal workers. Later, in the 15th and 16th centuries, our sources become much more plentiful and include listings of occupational fines giving us a much clearer idea of the available specialisms. Moreover, this was at a time which nationally showed a growing demand for consumer goods.[103] The most important industry was that of cloth which dominated the economy of the town and its hinterland. But the urban character of Basingstoke could also be seen in the wide range of manufacturing occupations in metal, leather, and clothing, with specialist occupations such as smith, fletcher, glover and hosier (Fig. 9; appendix). It should be noted however, there were generally few in each occupation and this was a very different situation to great provincial towns, such as Salisbury and Winchester, which catered for a wider range of specialist occupations with sufficient numbers to allow organisation into guilds.[104]

Most of these other crafts fell within the mid-range of assessments. The few who paid at the minimum rate were a tailor, three barbers, and building craftsmen (a tiler and two carpenters). The rich were very much concentrated in the cloth industry, which catered for a much wider national and international market, but a few of the individuals or families who dealt with consumer goods made it into the ranks of the rich or the influential leaders of the town.

One such family was the Canners. John Canner was fined as a chandler in 1448, 1470 and 1491. Nicholas Canner was under-bailiff in 1464 and in 1481 was one of the most highly assessed citizens only six being above him, while in 1464/5 Thomas Canner sold tallow and wax candles. They were also probably part of a family of substantial farmers in neighbouring Mapledurwell.[105] Later, another Thomas Canner was born in Basingstoke before making a career for himself in the academic world of Oxford (see below, p. 74).

Tailors and Clothing

The 15th and 16th centuries saw the growth of the tailoring industry both here and elsewhere.[106] As the town prospered, the demand for such consumer goods grew. In some cases this was reflected in the sale of luxury imported cloths, headgear, and mercery,

---

102 *The Hampshire Tax List of 1327*, 70–1. There was also a Whitebred and a Chaplain.

103 M. Kowaleski, 'A consumer economy', in R. Horrox and W.M. Ormrod (eds), *A Social History of England, 1200–1500* (1996), 238–59; C. Dyer, *An Age of Transition: Economy and Society in England in the Later Middle Ages* (2005), 145–57; J. Hare, 'Production, specialisation and consumption in late Medieval Wessex', in L. Clark (ed.), *The Fifteenth Century XIV: Essays presented to Michael Hicks* (Martlesham, 2015), 189–206.

104 J. Hare, 'Salisbury: the economy of a fifteenth century provincial capital', *Southern History* 31 (2010), 4–5; C. Haskins, *The Ancient Trade Guilds and Companies of Salisbury* (Salisbury, 1912), 60–1; Keene, *Medieval Winchester*, ii.

105 It was evidently a family of note. Nicholas Canner was under-bailiff in 1464, and in 1481 only six men had an assessment greater than his. Thomas Canner was also in the same trade as John and sold tallow and wax candles in 1464.

106 Hare, 'Production, specialisation and consumption', 204.

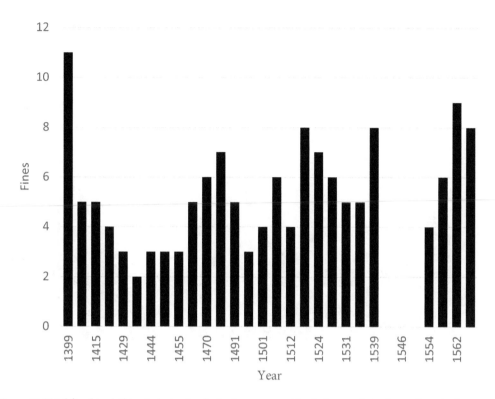

Figure 11 *Total fined in clothing industry (excludes those engaged in cloth manufacturing and marketing; most were tailors but with the occasional capper and hosier). Source: see appendix.*

such as recorded in Thomas Lane's inventory (see above, p. 50). Most of its luxury goods probably came from London, although some may have come from Southampton through Salisbury or Winchester. But other clothing consisted of tailored English cloth, now increasingly produced by specialist craftsmen using more specialist sewing techniques. The number of fines varied from year to year. These were particularly high in 1399, dropped in the early 15th century, recovered from the 1470s, and reached peaks in the period 1514–40 and late 16th century. Their absence in 1540–52 seems to represent a change of taxing policy towards the tailors rather than a sign of economic decline. Nevertheless, while the industry probably flourished, its growth was nothing like that of Salisbury.[107] Basingstoke's hinterland was much smaller.

Leather Craftsmen

The leather industry was, after that of cloth, arguably the next most important manufacturing industry in the country, but here as elsewhere the documentation is poor.[108] There were concentrations of this industry in most small towns.[109] In addition

107 Hare, 'Production, specialisation and consumption', 204.
108 Hare, *Prospering Society*, 165–6.
109 For comparable figures in a neighbouring county see Hare, *Prospering Society*, 166.

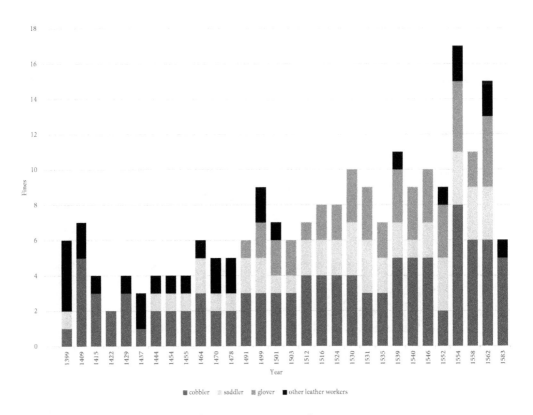

Figure 12 *The leather industry: numbers fined. Source: see appendix.*

the area around Basingstoke possessed a ready supply of hides, sheep and cattle, while the Hampshire basin was a substantial exporter of hides through Southampton.[110] The number of leather workers fined grew. It remained fairly steady in the 15th century, albeit with a drop in 1429–55, but generally about five to six leather workers were fined each year. There was a substantial rise to nine in 1499 with a further rise midway through the following century. Moreover, in the 16th century there was a growing number of specialist workers, described as cobblers, glovers or saddlers. It is not clear how far this was merely a representation of the occupational assessments and how far it was a sign of greater specialisation. But something of this specialisation can be seen in the need for regulations of the glovers, limiting the hours in which they could wash skins in the river.[111]

The glovers were not among the richest but they were often men of substance within the community. The Ronanger family had arrived as newcomers by 1478 when John was fined as a cobbler, as he was successively until 1516. He may have been the bailiff three times between 1509/10 and 1515/6, before dying in 1516. The next generation (John and Richard) moved into the mercery and drapery trade, but other members subsequently came back into the leather business with a saddler from 1524 to 1560. Richard atte Hore, was a glover who was a substantial mid-ranking figure in 1524. Something of Richard

110   Hare, *Prospering Society*, 166; Baigent & Millard, *Basingstoke*, 352–3.
111   Baigent & Millard, *Basingstoke*, 349.

Grow's substantial cobbler's business can be seen in his inventory in 1579, with his stock of 39 dozen pairs of shoes and five pairs of boots.[112]

Metal Goods

There were generally two or three men who were fined for trading in metal goods in the 15th century, with a gap when they were not fined in 1536–41, and then four or occasionally six from 1544. Virtually all were described as smiths. In addition, an occasional cutler and ironmonger were fined, and we also have someone described as a brazier in a title deed. In addition, some metal goods were dealt with by other traders. This can be seen in the trade in nails. When Gossmer, the vicar, wanted large quantities of nails, he did not use local smiths. Instead he went to two mercers, who presumably bought them in Southampton from among the Spanish imports. In addition, he acquired some from Reading and from a Dudley (Worcs.) man, the latter as a part of the influx of midland nails into this area also documented at Winchester College.[113]

The Building Industry

Basingstoke was a town of timber-framed buildings, and carpenters form the most frequent example from the building industry, with only occasional references to tilers and masons. However, carpenters are only sometimes listed amongst the occupations being fined, not in many years between 1485 and 1512, and rarely after 1514 (see appendix). For some reason it was then decided that they should no longer be fined. It is thus only for the early 15th century that we can generalise about this group. From 1399 to 1470 there were usually three to five carpenters (comparable to those in the large small towns of neighbouring Wiltshire),[114] with a minimum of two in 1409 and a maximum of eight in 1432 and 1437. Although we do not have records for every year, it is clear that we are dealing with men who were based in Basingstoke. Of the 35 known carpenters, eight were well-established and active for periods of between seven and 26 years.[115] As elsewhere carpenters could take on projects in the hinterland beyond the town, and carpenters from elsewhere could be employed in the town itself. We have no specific example of the latter, although we know that this could happen even in much larger towns or cities like Salisbury,[116] but a contract for £22, to build a new roof over the nave and a timber bell tower, at the small nunnery of Wintney was drawn up with two Basingstoke carpenters in 1415, and both are known from the town records.[117] William Austin, was described as a carpenter in 1409,[118] and fined as such in 1422.[119] He acted as a pledge in a legal dispute about land in the royal courts at Westminster in 1413 and

---

112 HRO, 1580A/39/1–2.
113 *English Inland Trade*, 164–5; C.U.L., MS Ll.2.2, 4r, 3r; W.A. Harwood, 'Trade and consumption patterns in central Southern England: The supply of iron and wax to Winchester College, c.1400–1560', *Southern History* 29 (2008), 7–10.
114 Hare, *Prospering Society*, 166–7.
115 7, 13, 15, 16, 19, 22, 22, 26 years respectively.
116 L.F. Salzman, *Building in England down to 1540: A Documentary History* (Oxford, 1952), 516–17.
117 Ibid., 492.
118 Baigent & Millard, *Basingstoke*, 253.
119 HRO, 148M71/2/7/1.

he became part of the governing elite of the town, serving as one of the two bailiffs in 1430–1.[120] John William, the other carpenter, was fined as a carpenter in both 1415 and 1422.[121] Another craftsmen producing for outside the town was the painter, Thomas Draycote, who, in 1424, painted the picture of St George for the free standing inn sign at the new inn in Alresford which had recently been rebuilt by Winchester College.[122]

Other Manufactures

The only other occupation that was usually fined were the chandlers, producing candles, to deal with the essential need for light. There were usually one or two fined in the 15th century, none between 1499 and 1531, and two to four from 1540 onwards. Other occupational fines were isolated and suggest individual year to year decisions by the assessors or the clerk. These included isolated fines on a wheelwright, a cooper and a fletcher. There were also a group of labourers who were fined each year, although it is not clear what they were doing.

The Service Sector: Barber, Religious, Lawyers, Attorneys

This group constituted isolated figures. The barbers or barber surgeons, first appear in the list of fines in 1478, and made up two or three individuals each year. There would be a small group of clerics serving the parish church, the chapel and the hospital. In the early 16th century, before the changes of the Reformation, the vicar and four clerics were recorded.[123] It is unlikely that there were any full-time lawyers in the town, but there were evidently men who could represent others in court and were described as attorneys, but were not fined as such.

The Town's Distant Trade

Basingstoke was for a long time the chief marketing centre for the area around, but it was also part of a pattern of long-distance external and international trade, in which it acted as a distribution point for the export of wool and later of cloth. Its export of wool also provided a means of bringing imported foreign products required by the citizens. Its two main outlets were the ports of Southampton and London. Southampton was a major port for trade with Normandy and Gascony, for the Mediterranean and for Spain.[124] London was a little further from Basingstoke than Southampton (48 miles and 30 miles respectively) but the capital also possessed a much more important port, the greatest in the country with a wider range of products than anywhere else, and London was also by

---

120   Baigent & Millard, *Basingstoke*, 257, 435.
121   HRO, 148M71/2/1/15; 2/7/1.
122   WCM, 1824.
123   HRO, 21M65 B1/1 f. 43r.
124   C. Platt, *Medieval Southampton: A Port and Trading Community, AD 1000–1600* (London and Boston, 1973), 69–77, 152–64.

far the most important cloth exporting port in the country, and growing in importance at the very time when the Basingstoke cloth industry was at its peak.[125]

Trade through Southampton

Southampton was an important port, handling about 14 per cent of the country's recorded trade in the early 13th century, and it was the second most important port after London by *c*.1480.[126] After London, it was the most important cloth exporting port for much of the 15th century.[127] We have little evidence of specific Basingstoke trade in the 13th century. In part this may have reflected the town's involvement with larger intermediate trading points such as Winchester, and its great regional St Giles' fair. But we know that occasionally, at least, Basingstoke's merchants were engaged in direct trade with the ports and in the international trade. In the early 1270s, John Fynian and Edward Karite, two Basingstoke merchants were engaged in the wool trade, much at least through Southampton.[128] It was rare for such events to be documented, moreover there was likely to have been additional trade between town and port, which was finally exported by others in the port. These few examples therefore suggest that Basingstoke was a focus for a much more extensive long distance trade in wool.

We know much more about Basingstoke's trade with Southampton in the 15th and 16th centuries, than at other times, thanks to Southampton's remarkable brokage books. These unique documents recorded with considerable detail the goods leaving the town of Southampton. They list the goods, where they were going and when, who carried them and who owned them.[129] There are nothing like them for any other port and they can be used to shed much light on Basingstoke's evolving trade. Carts to Basingstoke had been relatively few and relatively stable in numbers during the 15th century, with a peak of thirteen carts in 1440 but there were substantially more in the early 16th century. The growth of the town and the cloth industry seems to have encouraged direct trade to Southampton rather than using intermediate markets such as Winchester or Salisbury.

During the 15th century, the main recorded item of direct trade to Basingstoke was wine, which made up almost half the recorded transactions. Fish only made up a small part of the direct trade (six carts). The remaining transactions covered a variety of occasional items: iron, oil, cards, fruit, bowstaves, brass, wool and mill stones.[130] A mill stone would have been bought at the port when required, and one was bought in 1492 by John Kingsmill, one of the town's millers. By the 1520s and 1530s, Basingstoke's trade had grown substantially and rather changed in character. The number of carts had increased from an annual average of eight to 38 per year. Wine remained a substantial part of the trade with 19 per cent of the transactions, but fish became much more important

125 C. Barron, 'London 1300–1540', *CUHB*, 412–18.

126 M. Kowaleski, 'Port towns: England and Wales, 1300–1540', *CUHB*, 476–7.

127 Hare, 'Salisbury: The economy of a fifteenth-century provincial capital', 11; E.M. Carus-Wilson and O. Coleman, *England's Export Trade, 1275–1547* (Oxford, 1963), passim.

128 1271, 2, 3, 4 (Finian and Vyvyen); *Cal. Pat.* 1266–72, 555, 689; *Cal. Pat.* 1272–81, 36; Baigent & Millard, *Basingstoke*, 185. Both men are known as active in Basingstoke – see Baigent & Millard: for Fynian (*c*.1250–*c*.1280), 599, 600, and for Karite (*c*.1250–1274), 599, 600, 602–4, 605, 656.

129 M. Hicks and W.A. Harwood, 'Introduction', *English Inland Trade*, 1–10. The following paragraphs are based on *Overland Trade Database*.

130 For John Kingesmyll in 1491, one of the town's millers, see HRO, 148/2/7/9.

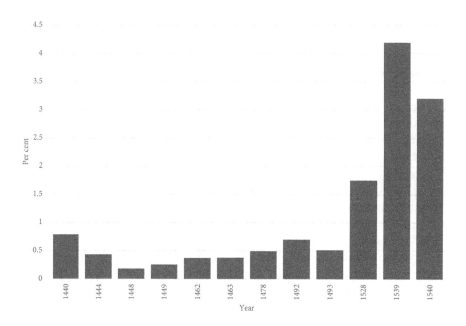

Figure 13 *Basingstoke's trade with Southampton: 1440–1540, expressed as a percentage of carts sent from Southampton. Sources: calculated from* English Inland Trade, *31, 97. Dates by close of accounting year.*

accounting for 63 per cent of transactions. The seven loads of woad, an essential dyestuff, reflect the growth in the cloth industry in the early 16th century. The two loads of hops probably indicate the growth of hop beer, with its longer life. Beer brewing was increasingly spreading among the towns of South East England in the later 15th and early 16th century as in Basingstoke (see above).[131] In addition there were single dispatches of oranges and raisins and five dispatches of iron.

Occasionally something more can be said about the men involved. In the 15th century they were usually involved in isolated transactions. The obvious exception was Julian of Basingstoke in 1440, who was engaged in five transactions of wine and one of oil, besides sending wine to Reading. Richard Kingesmill, a wealthy innkeeper from 1455–70, brought in fruit, fish and wine in 1462/3.[132] By 1565/6 the pattern of trade had changed dramatically. Southampton had lost most of its international trade, and its hinterland had contracted enormously. In the four months that were sampled, only four carts were sent to Basingstoke.[133]

In the 16th century, the growth of trade had led to some of the town's mercantile elite setting up family agents in the port, who became established Southampton merchants but maintained clear links with their home town. William Grete was a member of a long-standing Basingstoke family who had been amongst the wealthiest in the town in 1523 and part of the governing urban elite. He became a burgess of Southampton, where he concentrated on the fish trade. All his recorded trade with Basingstoke, which

131 M. Mate, *Trade and Economic Development 1450–1550* (Woodbridge, 2006), 62–5; see below.
132 See J. Hare, 'Inns, innkeepers and the society of later medieval England (1350–1600)', *Jnl of Medieval Hist.* 39 (2013), 91.
133 SAO, SC 5/5/52.

in 1538–40 averaged eleven transactions a year, were of fish. He also supplied fish
to Newbury and Winchester. Another probable relation, John Grete of Basingstoke,
imported salt in 1527/8 and the family continued in Basingstoke with William Grete,
draper. Robert Ronanger also came from a rich Basingstoke family. He averaged fifteen
transactions a year in the brokage books in 1538–40, of which 55 per cent were of wine,
but he diversified to include fish, woad, iron, salt and oranges. He was also a burgess of
Southampton, and by 1548 had become controller of the customs there. His predecessor
in Basingstoke, Richard Ronanger, was a rich mercer and fishmonger and one of the
wealthiest inhabitants in 1523. The combination of trading in cloth and fish was not
unusual. Sale of cloth generated money in the port which could then be used to buy fish
to take back to Basingstoke. Like the Gretes, the Ronangers included a Southampton
merchant and a Basingstoke citizen (see below). Others involved in the Southampton-
Basingstoke trade at the end of the period included John Lypeskome, who was also a
butcher who averaged 7½ transactions, all of which were in fish, in the same two years
(1539 and 1540) and William James, who was involved eight times in 1527–8, mainly
for wine but also including some fish and iron. Others, as before, were individual
transactions. For wine these included at least two innkeepers Couslade and John Kent
in 1527/8.[134]

Some carts carried goods for specific gentry households in the area, as with wine in
1440 for Lord Brocas of Beaurepaire, in Sherborne St John, miscellaneous household
goods in 1462 for Sir John Wallop of Farleigh Wallop, wine in 1539 for the Warehams at
Malsanger, or fish in 1540 for William Paulet, Lord St John (cr. Baron St John in 1539,
and Marquis of Winchester in 1551).[135] In these cases the goods would have not entered
the town's market.

Occasionally Basingstoke men were recorded as directly involved in cloth exports:
In 1539/40, Robert Walker sent 40 pieces of kersey to Southampton and in 1527/8
John Stocker sent 100 kerseys[136] but the Brokage Books rarely record the import to
Southampton of cloth except from London. Moreover, much of Basingstoke's cloth
would have gone to London which was by far the more important of the two as cloth
exporting ports.

The Trade with London

Without the brokage books, our knowledge of the London trade would be much more
limited. Given the relative importance of the two ports, the London trade was probably
more important and certainly we can see much evidence of the close association between
Basingstoke and London, reflecting the importance of this trade. London dominated
the cloth trade, exporting seven times as many Hampshire kersies as Southampton in
1565/6, and would have thus been of crucial importance to Basingstoke.[137] This close
association between the two towns may be seen in the ability of Basingstoke families to
set up their sons as apprentices to London merchants and thus open up a potential career

134 SAO, SC 5/5/33.50r1, 33.17r5; Hare 'Inns, innkeepers', 92–3.
135 *Overland Trade Database*; *ODNB*, s.v. Paulet, William, first marquess of Winchester (1474/5?–1572),
     administrator and nobleman (accessed 10 Jan. 2017).
136 SAO, SC 5/5/33.11v7.
137 Rosen, 'Winchester in transition', 149.

in the capital. James Lancaster apprenticed two sons, James and Peter, to members of the Skinners' company in London. James became a freeman of London before making a new career and fortune in exploration, trading and naval warfare, while Peter ended up as second warden of the Skinners' Company.[138] James Deane whose family were already important figures in the Basingstoke cloth industry ended up as master of the London Drapers' company, an alderman of the city of London, as well as being knighted.[139] Another representative who established himself in London was Richard Yeates, who was already dead in 1618, when he was described in James Lancaster's will as 'late of London', but who was the son of two members of leading clothing families of Basingstoke: Agnes Lancaster and Richard Yates.[140] Anthony Puckeridge was apprenticed to a London haberdasher.[141] Another will refers to a Thomas Payne, clothier of Basingstoke, and a Robert Payne of London.[142] Other evidence of links between the town and capital can be seen in the debts of London merchants recorded in Basingstoke inventories. A mental orientation towards London is also reflected by William South, a dyer, from 1485 to 1523, who left a bequest to the Mount of Calvary in London in 1535.[143]

Although we cannot quantify the range of goods imported into the town, or distinguish between which came from London and which from Southampton, the range of luxury goods available may be seen in the contents of a single albeit exceptional inventory, listing the contents of the shop of Thomas Lane who died in 1532.[144] Thomas Lane was amongst the very rich of the town, a bailiff in 1524, and fined as a mercer in 1524 and 1530. There were spices: sugar, pepper, cinnamon, cumin, aniseed, ginger, saffron, nutmeg and 'vynecrek', brought from the Mediterranean and beyond. There were items of clothing: straw hats, men's shirts, Osnabruck headlak and diaper, girdles and hadlenbond, taps, together with the accessories pins, buckles and clasps, pouches and purses. There were matins books and ABC books, playing cards (coarse and fine), glue, a bundle of brown paper and a ream of white paper, pens and inkhorns. There were different types of cloth: vitry and course canvas, fustian, buckram, holland cloth, velvet, trench cloth and sackcloth. There were different types of thread: packthread, weak yarn, black thread and white thread, and sewing silk. There was a mixture of miscellaneous goods, from wedding rings and white plates, to soap from Castile and mercury or quicksilver. The mercers were exceptionally wealthy and there were few of them in the town, but Richard Ronanger had an even higher assessment in 1524. Above all, the inventory at least shows something of the range of goods available in the town. Lane's inventory is exceptional but not his wealth (see below, p. 59). Some, at least, of his goods could have come from Southampton, but most of these items were not sent direct to Basingstoke and probably were brought direct from London. Mercers also imported more basic products from the port: fish and nails. The fishmongers have been discussed

138 *ODNB*, s.v. Lancaster, Sir James (1554/5–1618), merchant, (accessed 4 Jan. 2017); M. Franks, *The Basingstoke Admiral: a life of Sir James Lancaster, c.1554–1618* (2006), 137, 201; J.J. Lambert, *Records of the Skinners of London: Edward I to James I* (1933), 294, 6, 7, 9, 301.

139 A.H. Johnson, *The History of the Worshipful Company of the Drapers of London*, ii (1915), 472; iii (1922), 82.

140 Franks, *Basingstoke Admiral*, 201.

141 HRO, 1574B/136.

142 HRO, 1596AD/81.

143 HRO, 1534B/34.

144 HRO, 1532B/09; I have sought to provide an indication of the range of goods rather than a comprehensive list.

elsewhere (see above). But when Richard Gosmer, the vicar, wanted nails for building works, he went to two mercers, Robert Stocker and John Belchamber, not to the local iron smiths.[145]

The Distance Trade Elsewhere

Much trade inevitably remains unrecorded, but occasionally the trading activities of the town's merchants and those of Southampton and London were amplified by the activity of other outsiders: John a Port and Thomas Coke were both leading merchants of Salisbury who brought wine for Basingstoke from Southampton in 1440 and 1492 respectively. These accounts also record an Andover merchant who imported fish in 1492, or merchants of Devizes and Winchfield who brought in oil for the town in 1462 and 1540 respectively.[146]

The town may also be seen as significant in the trade from further north and west. The Lancaster family was a newcomer family, perhaps from the north-west as their name may imply. The presence of such trade with this area may be reinforced by the debt owed by John Lancaster of Overton, a member of the prominent Basingstoke family, to a Kendalman. In 1583, William Crome, woollen draper owed money to Thomas Harryson, Kendalman, presumably for the purchase of cloth. Kendalmen, from the Lake District in the far north-west of England, were also regular visitors to Southampton in the early 16th century.[147]

The presence of trade with Wales and the Welsh March is also suggested by membership of the fraternity of the Holy Ghost in *c.*1460 by John Davy of Wales and David, merchant of Brecon.[148] Immigration also occurred from further afield. Basingstoke and its surrounding hundred saw a significant concentration of resident immigrants in 1440, but it is not clear from the records where most came from and this was probably before the great expansion of the town towards the end of the century.[149]

Town and Countryside

One of the difficulties in examining a medieval town is that by its very nature, it cannot be seen in isolation from the area around. Towns depended on the countryside and vice versa. In the pre-industrial age the town's immediate hinterland provided food and raw materials while the countryside depended on the towns for some of the specialist crafts and goods sourced from a distance. The growth of the cloth industry made Basingstoke even more dependent on the parishes immediately around than before, for cloth production as well as food. It was an economic relationship but also a social one. As Everitt commented on the market towns of Tudor England, 'The market town was

145 C.U.L., MS Ll.2.2.f.4r.
146 *Overland Trade Database.*
147 HRO, 1562/P/4/1; J. Hare, 'Southampton's trading partners: beyond Hampshire and Wiltshire', *English Inland Trade*, 110.
148 HRO, 148M71/5/1/1.
149 J.A. Lutkin, 'A survey of the resident immigrants in Hampshire and Southampton, 1330–1550', *PHFC* 70 (2015), 161, 155–68.

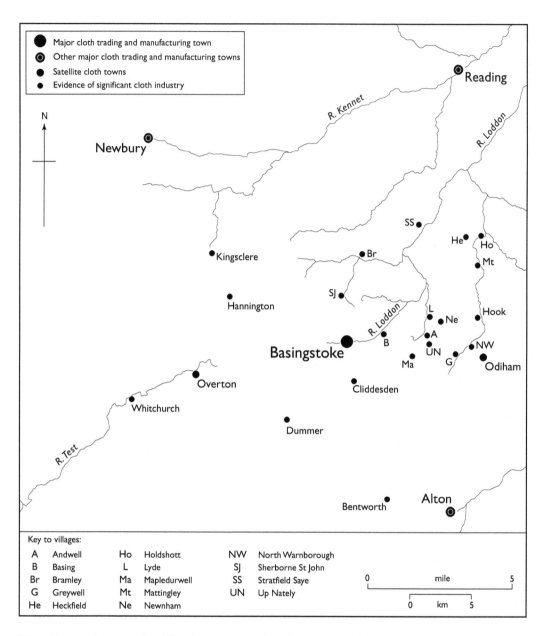

Map 6 *Town and country: the cloth industry, c.1500. The concentration to the east of Basingstoke in part reflects the concentration of research.*

not simply a centre of trade: it was the focus of the rural life around it.'[150] This section explores the vital economic relationship between town and countryside.

As we have seen there was already a market in Domesday Book and while some of this might have been for the distance trade, much of its activity would have been

150 A. Everitt, 'The marketing of agricultural produce' in J. Thirsk (ed.), *The Agricultural History of England and Wales IV, 1500–1640* (Cambridge, 1967), 488.

more local. The relationship remained poorly documented in the 13th century. In 15th and 16th centuries, the growth of the cloth industry added to the inter-relationship between town and country. Cloth was increasingly produced in the countryside and then marketed and sometimes finished in the towns. The dependence of the town on the countryside around was shown in the urban evidence (see above). There were evidently textile craftsmen among the urban population, as seen in the 23 weavers who were fined in 1524, but they tended to be among the poorer or mid-range assessments, representing small-scale independent producers. Many more were engaged in trading and finishing the cloth – much more than would be needed to be serviced by these urban weavers. Thus there were three mercers, five drapers, 28 fullers and five dyers compared with the 23 weavers. The town, its rich merchants and townsmen evidently depended on the production of the countryside beyond. This was apparent to contemporaries and in a petition of the clothiers in 1631 they claimed that 80 villages were dependent on the industry. The figure may be an exaggeration but nevertheless reflects the presence of large scale rural industry.[151] The process was an interaction between town and country in both ways. Some rural merchants operated on a large scale and could occasionally be found purchasing from urban merchants, rather than the other way around.[152]

Although the evidence for the rural cloth industry is scattered among many fragmentary sources, a cursory survey of evidence can demonstrate the importance of this industry in the area around (Map 6). A damaged, undated but mid 16th-century, source provides a listing of clothiers who were 'makers of fine kersies' in Hampshire, Berkshire, Surrey and Sussex. The Basingstoke area figures prominently including Overton (four names), Kingsclere (three), Whitchurch (four), Odiham (three), Greywell (one), Mattingley (three), Basingstoke (eight), and Andwell (two).[153] *Inquisitions post mortem*, occasional deeds and manorial accounts allow the production of lists of fulling mills, which increasingly became the focus of the rural industry. Finally wills and inventories can provide relevant information about the industry.[154]

There was a dye works at Sherborne St John in 1473.[155] The same village acquired a new fulling mill when John Kingsmill took an 80 year lease including an agreement to build a fulling mill in 1505.[156] Some others were also new as at Overton in 1431.[157] There were other fulling mills, especially in the valleys of the rivers Loddon, Lyde and Whitewater, at Andwell, Newnham, Stratfield Saye, Bramley, Hook and Heckfield.[158] Each mill serviced many weavers, and they were centres of activity. Thus at Andwell, the Milton family ran the mill. William Milton held 1½ virgates at his death by 1491 and

151 J. Thirsk and J.P. Cooper (eds), *Seventeenth Century Economic Documents* (1972), 38–9.

152 C.U.L., MS Ll.2.2.f.8r.

153 TNA, E 101/347/101.

154 For the wills and inventories the coverage has been comprehensive for period up to 1600 in Mapledurwell, Up Nately, Nately Scures, Newnham, Steventon and for those likely families in some other places.

155 Montagu Burrows, *The Family of Brocas of Beaurepaire and Roche Court* (1886), 393.

156 HRO, 31M57/35.

157 The first year of the lease was in 1430–1. There was no indication of it in the earlier accounts, while the lease continued in 1454/5. HRO, 11M59/B1/174; 173; M. Page (ed.), *The Pipe Roll of the Bishopric of Winchester* (Winchester, 1999), 213; HRO, 11M59/B1/191.

158 WCM, 3092, 25757–63; *VCH Hants* IV, 47, 107, 142, 157. For John Lyde of Newnham, fuller see HRO, 44M69/D1/6; *CIPM*, XVIII, 360.

was recorded in the Basingstoke court as early as 1465.[159] John Milton was recorded as a clothman in the period 1493–1500 and died in 1521.[160] Another John Milton (perhaps his son) was among the leading figures in the village, with the fourth highest assessed wealth in the village in 1525. He died in 1541,[161] but his widow continued the business. She was subsequently recorded among the makers of fine kersies.[162] She leased the fulling mill with her son Roger in 1542, by herself in 1545, and with her son Nicholas in 1560. Before her death in 1573 she still dwelt in the fulling mill.[163] Another wealthy branch of the family, with William Milton, was in neighbouring Basing, where William Milton was one of the two men most highly assessed on goods in 1525, and he was evidently actively involved in the cloth industry.[164]

In addition to rural villages, the cloth industry established itself in a series of satellite towns, particularly Odiham and Overton, which retained close links with Basingstoke. Odiham was already linked with Basingstoke by the aulnager in his 1467 account. Thomas Kitson, a very prominent London merchant born in Lancashire, bought cloth extensively from two Odiham clothiers in 1531.[165] Overton had acquired a new fulling mill.[166] Its close association with Basingstoke and with the smaller town's immediate hinterland is reflected in the will of John Lancaster of Overton, draper in 1562.[167] He was the son of Richard Lancaster of Basingstoke, one of two new recruits and wealthy drapers in Basingstoke (see below).[168] His second wife was the widow of another prominent Basingstoke clothing family, the Deanes. His witnesses included Rumblow Wadlow and Richard Denby. Rumblow, or his son with the same name, subsequently moved to Basingstoke and became a wealthy innkeeper (see below, p. 69). Meanwhile the Denbys reflect Overton's links with its own rural hinterland. They were notable figures in the area being among the most highly taxed figures in nearby Steventon in 1524–5, and Rumbold Denby was a clothier at Overton.[169]

The evidence of wills and inventories also makes clear the presence of the industry in neighbouring villages in the 16th century. At Greywell, Robert Chapman was described as a clothier when he died in 1524, and the family's wealth was reflected in the large number of wealthy Chapmans in the subsidy assessment.[170] When Thomas Chapman died in 1558, his inventory valued his goods and debts at over £300 including £123 in the wool loft.[171] At Mattingley, there were at least three clothier families.[172] At Basing,

159   WCM, 2917, 9; HRO, 148M71/2/1/63.
160   WCM, 29218 a; TNA, C 1/216/7 1493–1500 (catalogue).
161   HRO, 1541U/52.
162   TNA, E 101/347/17 (undated, mid 16th century – post 1541, probably *c.*1550, judging from the Basingstoke names).
163   WCM, 25757; HRO, 1573B/090.
164   TNA, E 179/173/183; HRO, 1542B/33.
165   P.H. Ramsey, *The Merchant Venturers in the First Half of the Sixteenth Century* (unpublished Univ. of Oxford D.Phil. thesis, 1958), 184; *ODNB*, s.v. Kitson, Sir Thomas (1485–1540), merchant and local politician, (accessed 10 Jan. 2017).
166   HRO, 11MS9/B2/27/2 & 3.
167   HRO, 1562P/4/1.
168   HRO, 1522B/14.
169   Morrin, *Steventon*, 40, 55; HRO, 1569P/06.
170   TNA, E 179/173/183.
171   HRO, 21M65/D3/80.
172   HRO, 10M64/73; 1545B/131; 1552B/088/2; 1576B/091, 1580A/78, 1582B/46/1.

apart from William Milton, there was another cloth trader, who bought 22 kerseys from a Basingstoke producer and trader.[173] Moreover, once inventories become available we see further evidence of rural industry as at Mapledurwell, Newnham, Up Nately and Cliddesden, with workshops containing looms or fulling and finishing equipment, debts for wool and oil, and a significant number of spinning wheels.[174]

The prosperity brought to the countryside was also reflected in its surviving church buildings. Although this was not an area of great cloth churches, such as Somerset or Suffolk, there was evidently considerable church building taking place. In these small parishes, the core of the church seems to remain that of 12th or early 13th centuries, until restored in the 19th century. But two features seem to be fairly general: a new roof was added in 15th or early 16th century, as at Mapledurwell, Newnham, Up Nately and Dummer, while in this area most churches were also given a new timber bell tower, added within the shell of the church. Few have been dated but that at Mapledurwell has been tree-ring dated to 1490–1522. At Up Nately the new roof was evidently associated with the, now, lost tower. At Mattingley, a remarkable timber-framed and brick church was constructed in the late 15th or early 16th centuries.[175] The earlier mother churches, were already much larger than these small parish churches, but they too saw considerable activities, as at Odiham, Overton and Basing.[176] This was an area where many new houses were built, in the countryside and amongst the associated satellite cloth towns such as Odiham. One notable example is provided at North Warnborough, where a long terrace of cottages of nine bays was built shortly after 1477/8 with an extension of another seven bays in after 1534/5, both facing the former common. Curiously only one bay seems to have been provided with any heating. Might this have been to reduce the fire risk in a building associated with cloth marketing?[177]

Town and countryside were closely integrated. This is reflected in the wills of some of the rich merchants whose bequests to neighbouring churches show a concern for the area around which would have been part of their economic world. Thus Edward Cook, an early mercer, who left bequests to Basingstoke church and chapel, also left bequests to the churches of Basing, Cliddesden, Farleigh, Wootton, Sherborne St John, Monk Sherborne, New Alresford and one other.[178] As elsewhere, the industrial wealthy sometimes migrated to the countryside.[179] Merchant families from Basingstoke moved into the adjacent countryside, as with the Kingsmills to Ashe and Sydmonton, the

---

173 C.U.L., MS Ll.2.2.f.8r.

174 Mapledurwell, 42; see also drafts by Hare, Morrin and Waight, on Up Nately and Andwell: https://www.victoriacountyhistory.ac.uk/counties/hampshire (accessed 4 Jan. 2017) and HRO, 1572B/060.

175 Hare 'Four churches from North East Hampshire: Mapledurwell, Newnham, Up Nately and Nately Scures', HFC Newsletter 62 (2014), 3–5; Pevsner, North Hampshire, 239, 392; Mapledurwell, 76, 78.

176 A new church tower was being built in the 1540s probably with stone from Titchfield Abbey, see J. Hare, The Dissolution of the Monasteries in Hampshire (Winchester, 1999), 23; HRO, 1541U/58; 1542U/08, 1543U/2; on Basing see J. Crook, 'New light on the history of St Mary's Church, Old Basing, Hampshire: an incised design for a post-medieval window', Jnl of the Brit. Arch. Assoc. 154 for 2001 (2002), 92–133.

177 Hare, 'Regional prosperity in fifteenth-century England: some evidence from Wessex', 112–13; Roberts, Hampshire Houses, 238; E. Roberts and D. Miles, 'Castle Bridge Cottages, North Warnborough, Hampshire', Vernacular Architecture 28 (1997), 117.

178 HRO, 1495B/1.

179 As with the Dolmans from Newbury to nearby Shaw. M. Yates, Town and Countryside in Western Berkshire, c.1327–c.1600: social and economic change (Woodbridge, 2007), 94.

Belchambers to Cliddesden, and the Deanes into Newnham, but it was an interaction that could be continuous and that also sucked in the adjacent country folk into the growing urban industry. The Stockers were agriculturalists in the area before becoming cloth merchants in the town (see below, pp. 63–4). The Canners remained important tenants and freeholders of Mapledurwell while becoming temporarily important townsmen. As late as 1594, the demesne lessee of neighbouring Andwell reflected these dual urban and rural family traditions. Gilbert Locker, a rich gentleman from a family of wealthy Basingstoke fullers, who possessed land in Andwell and Basingstoke, left his body to be buried in Basingstoke itself in, unusually, the school house, which before the Reformation had been the Holy Ghost chapel, upon which the citizens had lavished considerable wealth. Locker reminds us of the dangers of seeing towns in isolation. Towns and countryside were both economically and personally inter-twined and were part of a single world.

The Social Structure of the Town

MEDIEVAL SMALL TOWNS such as Basingstoke included a wide range of wealth, from rich to poor. This can be shown by the evidence of tax assessments, although these possess profound difficulties with their accuracy. Moreover, they do not cover all or even a fixed proportion of the urban inhabitants. This is clearly seen in the number of those assessed, which does not fit with any likely population trends. In the year 1327, 66 people were assessed, 132 in 1481, 279 in 1523, and only 50 in 1586.[1] Whatever happened in the 16th century, the population of the town did not fall by 72 per cent between 1523 and 1586. The most comprehensive assessment is clearly that for 1523–5.[2] Tax assessments are more valuable if they can be compared with evidence of occupations, such as is provided by the occupational fines of the 15th and early 16th centuries. Here again an analysis of the evidence in 1523–5, when the town was at the peak of its prosperity, seems particularly useful.

Nevertheless the earliest tax assessment in 1327, at least, shows that there was already a considerable diversity in taxable wealth. Of 66 taxpayers 13 paid the basic 7d., eight between 1s. and 2s. 9d., 15 between 3s. and 3s. 6d. and five above the latter figure. The maximum assessments were those of William le Forester and John Prat at 4s. 6d., nine times the basic payment

The basis of this section is provided by comparing the subsidy returns of 1523 with the court and estreat rolls for the town which list the fines imposed by the courts, above all with those of 1516 and 1524. These fines provide an indication of their occupations and survive from 1399, although not continuously. While they may not provide a complete coverage, they seem regular enough to suggest that they represent a licence to pursue an occupation rather than committing a specific offence (see above, p. 23). The number of those fined doubled from 78 in 1399 to 158 in 1524. Like most of our sources the figures need to be used with care. We should not treat any single year's list in isolation, and decisions about whether a particular occupation should be fined could change; nevertheless, they provide a potentially valuable source for long term trends. Of the 280 people assessed for the 1523 subsidy, 78 (28 per cent) can be provided with an occupation from the fines in 1524, allowing an analysis of occupations for almost a third of the taxpayers, at a time when the town was probably at the peak of its importance. The discrepancy between the lists of fines and assessments would be the result of a variety

1   *Hampshire Tax List of 1327*, 70–1; Baigent & Millard, *Basingstoke*, 393–5; *Hampshire Subsidy Rolls*, 39–40.
2   *Reg. Distr. Wealth, 1524–5* (for the detailed analysis, I have used the 1523 listing in the borough records: HRO, 148M71/3/4/2).

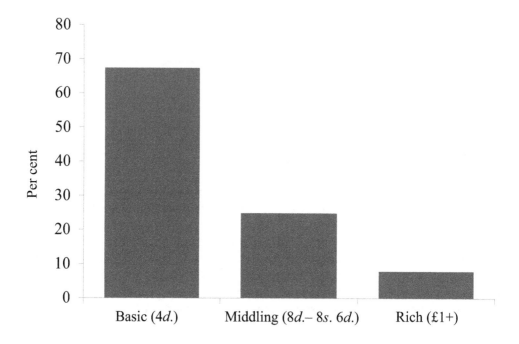

Figure 14 *Tax assessments, 1523. Source: HRO, 148M71/3/4/2.*

of factors. Many occupations, such as agricultural pursuits, were not fined, mortality and mobility might prevent a matching of the two sources, as would the use of different names or aliases for the same person or widely different spellings. However, this still leaves a substantial group where wealth and occupation can be correlated.

The taxpayers of 1523 have been divided into a simple threefold division by wealth: the rich, the middling sort and those who paid the minimum standard payment. In addition, there was a fourth group, those who did not pay tax and who probably came predominantly, but not exclusively, from the poor. They were unrecorded and must therefore be excluded from the analysis.

The group described here as the rich made up 20 (8 per cent) and have been distinguished as having a payment of £1 or more. This seems to be a clearly distinct group, given that no-one paid between 8*s.* 6*d.* and £1. The 63 (23 per cent) of the middling sort are thus distinguished by paying more than 4*d.* and not more than 8*s.* 6*d.* Most fell in the middle of this range with few payments at 8*d.* or 1*s.* and 50 of the group paying between 1*s.* 6*d.* and 5*s.* The largest group were those who paid the minimum 4*d.*, and constituted 171 tax payers (61 per cent). Although these will be described as poorer or basic taxpayers, they included independent craftsmen and probably the sons of the wealthy, such as William Belchamber, son of John.

John Ronanger was among the richest group. What is not clear is whetherJohn Ronanger, saddler, recorded 1516–31, can be identified with John Ronanger, a clothier noted in 1534. He has been included as a saddler in this table.

1523: Occupations					
Occupations		Total with occupation	Rich	Middling sort	Basic taxpayer
Cloth	Mercer	3	3	0	0
	Draper	5	2	3	0
	Fuller	23	7	9	7
	Weaver	13	0	4	9
	Dyer	4	0	2	2
Food	Baker	4	0	4	0
	Brewer	4	0	4	0
	Tapster/Taverner	14	0	6	8
	Fishmonger	2	2	0	0
	Butcher	2	1	1	0
	Miller	1			1
Services	Innkeeper	3	3	0	0
	Barber	5	0	2	3
Manufacturing	Glover	1	1	0	0
	Saddler	2	1	1	0
	Shoemaker	1	0	1	0
	Tailor	5	0	3	2
	Carpenter	2	0	0	2
	Tiler	1	0	0	1
	Smith	1	0	1	0
Labourers		9		2	7

Table 2 *Occupations in the tax assessment of 1523. Source: HRO, 148M71/3/4/2; 2/7/17, 2/7/18. Occupations taken from 1516 and 1524 fines. Some individuals were given more than one occupation.*

The Rich

The wealthiest were dominated by the cloth industry, with 11 of 19 from this group. At the head were the mercers, and in the 1524 subsidy, the four mercers, Richard and John Ronanger, Robert Pether and Thomas Lane, were assessed at payments between £1 10s. and £3 6s., and were all evidently men of wealth.[3] The inventory of the goods of Thomas Lane who died in 1532, shows the wide range of their activities (see above,

3   HRO, 148/M71/2/7/18; 148/M71/3/4/2; 148M71/2/7/5 & 7.

p. 50).[4] He also possessed links to other leading figures like Belchamber and Canner (see below). John Boyer, another mercer who had recently died, showed many of these same features (see above).[5] John Belchamber was another wealthy mercer and the richest of the innkeepers in 1523, being assessed at the highest figure of £80. He had been a long-established member of the urban elite. A William Belchamber was a miller in the town in 1443–8 and was involved in a debt case in 1450.[6] A John Belchamber was active until his death in 1513: he was highly assessed in the subsidy of 1481, was bailiff up to five times from 1485 to 1512, a tenant in 1487, a fishmonger and mercer in 1503 and 1512, possessed a fulling mill, and at his death bequeathed the large sum of £20 to the rebuilding of the church, making reference to payments from the Bell (probably an inn).[7] John Belchamber, his successor had been educated at Winchester College, returned to the family business, and was recorded as a mercer from 1515/6 until 1540. He was an innkeeper in 1524, but not in 1523 or in 1530. He served the town as baliff, the crown as tax collector, and the parish as church warden (see below, p. 70). After his death (in 1542), he was described as a clothier, but had already migrated from the town and returned to the neighbouring village of Cliddesden, where his descendants were still present in the 17th century.

The fullers were also prominent among the rich, although they ranged widely from rich to standard payers, and they included three of the five highest taxpayers: Robert Stocker, John Bye and the recently deceased Richard Deane[8] (see below). Other rich fullers were William Locker, Henry Lee and John Walker. Two of the drapers also come into this rich category, Hugh Lancaster and John Hoskyns, although none were among the very richest. A few other traders fell into the rich group, although they may have also been involved in wider trading.[9] The only three innkeepers whose assessment can be ascertained also fell into this category and there was also a butcher, William Grete.

The Middling Sort

This sector was also dominated by the cloth industry. There were a large number of fullers (25 were fined in 1516, 27 in 1523, 31 in 1524).[10] Although nine fell into this middling group, they ranged widely in wealth, from independent basic taxpayers to the very rich entrepreneurs who dominated the town. The Kingsmills provided a longstanding wealthy family, one branch of which had gone from innkeeper to become a royal justice and a member of the rural gentry. Another branch of the family had been engaged as fullers from mid century, one had been a fuller (and brewer) in 1455 and a fuller in 1470, and had invested in a new fulling mill in the countryside around.[11] They remained important figures in the community, albeit not among the

4   HRO, 1532B/09.

5   HRO, 148M71/2/7/9, 2/7/16; Baigent & Millard, *Basingstoke*, 436; Mag. Coll., 56/1EL1 f79 (catalogue).

6   HRO, 148M71/2/1/58 m. 5.

7   Baigent & Millard, *Basingstoke*, 395; 90–1 (although some of the latter entries may relate to the second John Belchamber); HRO, 148M71/2/7/16, 2/1/65; HRO, 1513B/1, TNA, PROB 11/18/3.

8   John Bye, Robert Stocker, the goods of a dead fuller held for his children; the other two were John Belchamber, innkeeper, and William Mores a gentleman.

9   A Richard Lancaster was a draper the previous year. John Hoskyns was already a draper in 1503.

10   HRO, 148M712/2/7/17, 2/1/65, 2/7/18.

11   See above, 53; HRO, 2/7/4, 2/7/7, HRO, 31M57/35.

wealthiest, and one assessed at 5s. came into our mid-range John Kingsmill fuller (or a father and son) was bailiff, four times between 1503 and 1510.[12] In 1524, a Richard Kingsmill was a fuller, and another member of the family was a miller, although with a much smaller assessment.[13] In addition, there were two drapers, four weavers (although mainly in the middle of this section) and two dyers in this category. Such men may have been engaged in trading, but they were essentially independent craftsmen rather than rich entrepreneurs. This group also included significant number of manufactures and those engaged in the food industry. There was a butcher, [a glover?], a saddler, three tailors and a smith, two barbers and one whose occupation was unknown. In the food industry all four bakers came into this category as did all four brewers, and almost half (six out of 14) of the taverners or tapsters (the rest being made up by basic taxpayers).

The Poorer Basic Taxpayers

This included small-scale independent producers. Again the cloth industry was represented. Twelve out of the 18 weavers were assessed at the minimum level and there were two dyers.[14] The fullers included some of the richest in the town, but they were also represented by seven basic taxpayers. Elsewhere these small craftsmen were represented in the food industry by eight tapsters/ taverners and a miller. The inclusion of a miller may seem surprising given the millers' grasping reputation and the capital requirements of a water mill, but there was at least one horse mill in the town, and this may have allowed smaller-scale provision. Among the service and consumer sector were three barbers, two tailors, two carpenters and a tiler. All the labourers except for one fell into this group.

The Distribution of Wealth in the Later 16th Century

Later tax returns are of much less value since they only affected a much smaller part of the population, with only 50 assessed in 1586. The cloth industry was responsible for almost half of these (three mercers, three drapers and a clothier) and this number has been underestimated both by the movement of cloth families, like the Stockers, into the countryside, and by families who, like the Halles, had once been industrialists assessed on goods and were now assessed on land. There were also two millers and three innkeepers taxed together with three in the food industry and three in consumer manufactures.

The Social Structure of Power: The Bailiffs

Another way of examining urban society is to look at the occupational structure of the most important office in the town, that of the two bailiffs. These have been analysed for the period 1386–1590 in four broad periods. In the late 14th and early 15th centuries, few bailiffs can be provided with occupations. Although this was a period when fewer

12   HRO, 148M71/2/7/18; Baigent & Millard, 436 (1503–4, 1506–7, 1508–09, 1509–10).
13   HRO, 148M71/2/7/18.
14   HRO, 148M71/2/7/18.

people were fined, the paucity of occupational links is interesting and suggests less specialisation. Many were nevertheless tenants and present in an early 15th-century rental. Some at least were from families known from their activities elsewhere in the town, as with a Lockyer and a Pottinger. There were no clothworkers, although this industry was in its early stages of growth in the 1430s and 1440s. It was the latter part of the 15th century that was to see the transformation of Basingstoke into a cloth town and this was reflected in the occupations of the bailiffs, initially before 1490 and more so in the 16th century (see table 3). The cloth industry now dominated the posts of bailiff. There were occasional representatives of the food, consumer and service sectors, and people who came from landed or gentry backgrounds, but such examples were much less frequent. The rich dominated the post of bailiff, although this may have gone much further. In the much more restricted 1586 subsidy assessment the richest half accounted for all but one of the bailiffs.[15]

Date	No. of bailiffs	No. in cloth industry	Other occupation	Gent	Unknown	Comments
1386–1447	29	0	3	0	26	baker, carpenter, miller
1450–1490	17	5	3	1	9	2 innkeepers, 1 miller.
1490–1530	24	10	5	2	7	butcher, chandler, cobbler, saddler, miller
1530–1590	37	20	3	0	14	saddler, tailor, miller

Table 3 *Occupation of bailiffs. Source: Baigent & Millard*, Basingstoke, *434–8; for occupational fines see appendix. Occupations classified as in the cloth industry: mercers, drapers, fullers, clothiers, dyers. 1450–90: one man appears as both a mercer (1470, 1478, 1491) and a miller (1485), hence the discrepancy in the figures.*

Stability and Mobility

Traditionally towns had probably depended on an influx of newcomers, but this would particularly be the case at periods of expansion. The growth of the cloth industry in later 15th- and early 16th-century Basingstoke would have provided enormous opportunities, both for families existing in the town and the villages immediately around, and for those coming from further away. Something of this variety, and of how families used the opportunities, can be seen through examining a few case studies.

The Lockers had existed for a long time in the neighbouring village of Cliddesden, where they were probably among its leading families. They were here in the 13th century with an Adam le Lokere, and later in the restrictive tax assessment of 1327 there were two John Le Loquers.[16] In *c.*1353, Agnes, daughter of John Le Loukare of Cliddesden was seized, taken to Basing and raped.[17] The family remained in the village in the 15th century with two of them involved in a hue and cry in 1415, and presentments for

---

15　This included one person who held the post three times and one who held it twice. Calculated from Baigent & Millard, *Basingstoke*, 434–8 and *Hampshire Subsidy Rolls*, 39–40.

16　Baigent & Millard, *Basingstoke*, 601; *Hants Tax List 1327*, 20.

17　*Cal. Pat.* 1350–1354, 440. The reference comes from a pardon in 1353 to the parson of Farleigh for his involvement in the offence.

brewing here in 1399 and 1464.[18] But they also extended their activities into Basingstoke, where they came under the control of the town courts in the 1380s and in the early 15th century.[19] William Locker was fined for pasturing 60 sheep in 1426, is recorded as a tenant in 1464/5, was a wealthy tenant in 1481, a bailiff in 1446, and was sued by the vicar for debt in 1446, 1448 and 1455.[20] A John Looker also existed in neighbouring Basing c.1460.[21] The family seem to have made the most of the changing industrial and trading economy of the town. Gilbert flourished, from 1491 to 1508, as a mercer and brewer,[22] while a John was fined as a weaver in 1499 and 1523.[23] William, son of Gilbert, was active from 1523 to 1546, was already a fuller in 1524, and was one of the richest men in town in 1523. He became a mercer and fishmonger by 1531 and was a bailiff in 1541/2 and 1545/6.[24] At his death, the business was taken over by his widow Joanna from 1545 to 1560.[25] Gilbert, their successor, was described as a clothmaker in 1543, but died in 1558.[26] The family later moved out into the countryside and another Gilbert leased the demesne at Andwell from 1584, setting himself up as a country gentleman, although he still looked back to the town and the chapel of the Holy Ghost, where his father and mother were buried, for his own burial and spiritual home.[27] There was a fulling mill at Andwell, but this was distinct from the demesne lease and operated by someone else. His inventory shows his wealth and his role as a country gentleman, with his 302 sheep, 52 cattle, 18 horses and 50 pigs and £181 worth of crops, and a house with nine beds. Altogether his goods were assessed at £1,137 of which £600 lay in the value of his lease.[28]

The Stockers were another family who seem to have come from the immediate agrarian hinterland. John Stocker in 1442 was involved in farming in Eastrop, and was presented for taking sheep flocks back and forth between Basingstoke and neighbouring Eastrop. They also possessed their own sheep flock in 1481 and were substantial taxpayers.[29] William, one of these, and Juliana in c.1460 contributed to the guild of the Holy Ghost. Nicholas Stocker was the first to appear among the urban occupations, being fined as a fuller from 1470 to 1491, and he was also bailiff in 1511.[30] There may have then been two brothers, for a Robert exported cloth through Southampton in 1491, and Agnes Stocker, a widow who had taken over from her husband was fined as a fuller and baker from 1499–1501, while Nicholas was still alive.[31] The next generation included two powerful figures within the town. Robert was a fuller, clothier and brewer (from 1512 to

18   HRO, 148M71/2/1/15; 2/1/4; 2/1/63.
19   Baigent & Millard, *Basingstoke*, 222, 248–50.
20   Baigent & Millard, *Basingstoke*, 259, 295, 394, 276; D.G. Le Faye, 'Selborne Priory and the vicarage of Basingstoke', *PHFC* 46 (1990), 96; HRO, 2/1/51–5, 60, 2/7/5; Reg. Waynflete i 81v; Baigent & Millard, *Basingstoke*, 29, 116–17.
21   HRO, 148M71/5/1/1.
22   HRO, 148M71/2/7/9; 2/7/16; TNA, PROB 11/16/141.
23   HRO, 148M71/2/7/12; 2/7/18.
24   HRO, 148M71/2/7/18; 3/4/2; 2/7/19; Baigent & Millard, *Basingstoke*, 436.
25   HRO, 1560A/22.
26   Probably the son of William and Joanna, but there is no direct evidence.
27   Himsworth, *Winchester Coll.* II, 184, 186.
28   HRO, 1621B/31/2.
29   Baigent & Millard, *Basingstoke*, 273, 394–5.
30   HRO, 148M71/2/7/7, 2/7/8.
31   *Overland Trade Database*.

1539), who took cloth to Southampton in 1528, and was bailiff three times.[32] Meanwhile John Stocker was a fuller from 1516 to 1531.[33] At the same time Gilbert Stocker was fined as a clothier from 1534 to 1544, and died in 1563. He was a clothmaker and leased a tenement from Winchester College in 1533. He possessed the highest tax assessment in 1560, made one of the highest contributions for the reinstatement of the chapel and Fraternity of the Holy Ghost in 1557, and was bailiff four times between 1546 and 1562.[34] His brother Thomas was also a clothier.[35] Other members of the next generation included Robert, who rose from clothmaker to yeoman, and William, warden of the guild of the Holy Ghost in 1574.[36]

Another longstanding family were the Kingsmills, whose name derived from one of the town mills, although they had earlier moved out of the town. William Kingsmill was well-established and a bailiff of the town in 1390–1.[37] Subsequently Richard became a powerful innkeeper in the later 15th century, and his son rose through education to national prominence in the law, while another branch of the family became important figures in the town's cloth industry.[38]

Some families were long-standing in the town without being directly involved in the cloth industry, although no doubt also profiting from the prosperity that it brought. The Grete family long-remained as butchers, from 1398 until the mid 16th century, when they diversified by producing Southampton burgesses and, through education, a role in the church at Heckfield where a William Grete became vicar. (See above, pp. 40–1.)

It is more difficult to demonstrate an absence of a family than their presence, since the documentation cannot be expected to be comprehensive. But some notable families seem to have been newcomers who arrived from outside during the period of dynamic growth for the cloth industry, from the 1460s into the early 16th century. The Lancaster family provides an example of a late arrival that appears to have gone straight into the cloth industry. They were first fined in 1499 as drapers and as their name may suggest, they may have been part of a wider trade to the North West (see above, p. 51). Richard Lancaster was fined as a draper from 1499 to 1522 when he died.[39] Hugh, probably a brother, was the mid-range draper in the 1523 assessment, continuing as a draper from 1512, until his death in 1525.[40] Both Richard and Hugh produced several children, but the family then briefly disappeared from the occupational fines, suggesting that the sons were still children at the time of their fathers' deaths. Nevertheless, later another generation continued in business. James was fined from 1539 to 1546 as a draper,[41] and Richard, son of Richard, in 1534/5. James' family is shown in his widow Elizabeth's will,

32   HRO, 148M71/2/1/65–2/7/21; *Overland Trade Database*; Baigent & Millard, *Basingstoke*, 436–7.
33   HRO, 148M71/2/7/18; 2/7/20.
34   HRO, 148M71/2/1/66; 2/7/24; Himsworth, *Winchester Coll.* II, 186, 184; Baigent & Millard, *Basingstoke*, 397–8.
35   TNA, C 1/1144/19–21; HRO, 1547/B/81.
36   Himsworth, *Winchester Coll.* II, 187; Baigent & Millard, *Basingstoke*, 128; Millard, *Holy Ghost*, 2; HRO, 1576AD/52.
37   Baigent & Millard, *Basingstoke*, 434.
38   *ODNB*, s.v., Kingsmill family (*per. c.*1480–1698), gentry (accessed 11 Jan. 2017) and below, 73.
39   HRO, 148M71/2/7/12; 2/1/65; HRO, 1522B/14.
40   HRO, 148M712/2/1/65; 2/7/18; 1525B/09.
41   HRO, 148M71/2/7/21; 2/7/27.

with a John as the eldest son, but two other sons were apprenticed to London skinners.[42] The family, as we will see, also made use of education. Christopher, son of Hugh was sent to Winchester College in 1529. William, whether the son of Hugh or the first Richard, ended up as registrar of the bishop of Bath and Wells, and his three sons were all sent to Corpus Christi College, Oxford[43] during the tenure as warden of Thomas Greenway, a member of another Basingstoke family. The family also diversified economically. Another William Lancaster was fined from 1552 as a draper before shifting to be an innkeeper from 1558 to 1583, while another moved to Overton, a few miles to the west, where he set up himself in the cloth business.[44]

The Ronanger family were also outsiders who established themselves as wealthy merchants in the cloth industry, although in this case, first establishing themselves, and making their mark, in another trade. John was probably a newcomer and was fined from 1478 to 1516 as a cobbler, and had already been assessed above the very basic rate in 1481 and was bailiff in 1515/16.[45] Richard established himself as a mercer and merchant (1512–45).[46] Another John became a prominent member of the town as clothier, mercer and fishmonger and draper, bailiff and warden of the guild of the Holy Ghost, before dying in 1558.[47] He may, however, have begun as a specialist leather craftsman.[48] The next generation showed a shift back from the cloth industry and into consumer goods. John Ronanger, junior, returned to the family's activity in the leather industry as a saddler in 1539, 1558–60, and later another John was a tailor 1554–62 before dying in 1587.[49]

The Greenway family, was another that seems to have originated as newcomers who only later shifted into the cloth industry. They first appear as barbers, with Thomas fined in 1478.[50] A John Greenway paid tax in 1481 and continued as a barber until at least 1524, appearing with another John, junior, in 1516.[51] In 1524, in addition to this John, barber, John Greenway junior had become a chandler, and there was a Gilbert Greenway fuller, who paid the basic 4d. in taxation.[52] It is not clear which of these was the father of the Thomas who later became president of Corpus Christi College Oxford (see below, pp. 73–4). John Greenway, the younger, later rose to greater importance within the town, becoming a bailiff in 1568–9, warden of the Holy Ghost Guild in 1561, 1569 and 1570, to which he made one of the highest contributions to the fund for its restoration in 1557, and he was one of the most highly assessed men of the town in 1560. He was fined as a mercer and fishmonger in 1551 and 1552 and was described as a woollen draper in his

42 HRO, 1581B/68. James has described himself as a husbandman in 1571: M. Franks, *The Basingstoke Admiral: The Life of Sir James Lancaster* (2006), 180.

43 J.K. McConica and C.S. Knighton, 'Some sixteenth-century Corpus families: Kingsmills, Nappers, Lancasters and others', *The Pelican*, 1978–9, 6–9.

44 HRO, 148M71/2/7/30; 2/7/34; 2/7/35.

45 HRO, 148M71/2/7/8, 2/7/17.

46 HRO, 148M71/2/1/65; 2/7/17; 2/7/26.

47 HRO, 148M71/2/1/66, 2/7/27; Baigent & Millard, *Basingstoke*, 437; 1558B/199/1.

48 In 1516 John Ronninger, junior, was a saddler while another, but senior, remained as a cobbler. Between 1530 and 1534 the saddler was replaced by a clothier with the same name. HRO, 148M71/2/7/17; 2/7/19; 2/1/66.

49 HRO, 148M71/2/7/21; 2/7/34; 2/7/35; 2/7/33; 2/7/35; 1587AD62; Millard, *Holy Ghost*, 2.

50 HRO, 148M71/2/7/8.

51 HRO, 148M71/2/7/17; Baigent & Millard, *Basingstoke*, 395.

52 HRO, 148M71/2/7/18; 20.

will in 1578.[53] John Greenway was a cap maker in 1551. He may have been the former's son and rose to prominence in the 1580s, as bailiff in 1585–6, warden of the guild of the Holy Ghost in 1586, a mercer in 1581 and 1583, and was taxed on land in 1586.[54]

These families all maintained themselves within the town, and in the male line, for several generations. It was a closely-knit world. There was also considerable intermarriage between members of the wealthy elites. When John Ronanger the elder died in 1558 his daughters were married into other members of the cloth trading families: Hopkins, Yate and Pettie, while a Yate was married to a Pethys and a Grene.[55]

Inns and Innkeepers

Basingstoke was an important marketing and industrial centre on a major long-distance route from Salisbury and the West Country to London. As such it needed the provision of accommodation and inns for long-distance travellers and merchants who came to trade in the area. Hospitality for travellers must have been provided from an early date, but the specialist provision of inns was something that developed here, as elsewhere, in the 14th and 15th century.[56] Such inns filled a variety of functions. They provided overnight accommodation for those on long-distance routes, whether in private rooms or in the communal shelter of the hall, as well as the possibility of hiring horses. They provided hospitality for those traders who came from afar, particularly London, to trade in cloth. They provided places for informal trade, and their halls may well have served as a focus for social or administrative activity. In 1595, witnesses in a case before the Master of Requests were examined at the George.[57] The inn trade generated cash that could be reused to the benefits of the innkeepers, who were among the rich elite of the town. They provided a link between the distant and the local economies. Lords showed an awareness of the financial advantages of the inn trade and felt it worthwhile to invest heavily in their construction. Winchester College spent about £400 on its new Angel Inn at Andover, a similar-sized town to Basingstoke.[58]

Each year, there were generally three hostellers who were fined, for selling oat bread or horsebread or unspecified offences. Sometimes, this rose to four and very rarely to five. This seems to have become a general fine on the occupation, in effect, a licence to trade. Moreover, innkeepers were fined much more heavily than those in other occupations, apart from the bakers, as in 1454.[59] A list of inns compiled for the

---

53   HRO, 148M71/2/7/29; 2/7/30; Baigent & Millard, *Basingstoke*, 128, 438, 398; TNA, PROB 11/60/180; Millard, *Holy Ghost*, 230. To complicate matters in 1557 there were three John Greenways: a mercer, a draper and an elder: Millard, *Holy Ghost*, 2–3.

54   Baigent & Millard, *Basingstoke*, 438, 129; HRO 148M71/2/7/34; 2/7/35; *Hampshire Subsidy Rolls*, 39–40; Millard, *Holy Ghost*, 2–4; TNA, PROB 11/60/180.

55   HRO, 1558B/199/2; 1580A/99.

56   J. Hare, 'Inns, innkeepers and the society of late medieval England', *Jnl of Medieval Hist.* 39 (2013), 477–97.

57   Baigent & Millard, *Basingstoke*, 564.

58   J. Hare, 'Winchester College and the Angel Inn, Andover: a 15th century landlord and its investments', *PHFC* 60, 2005, 189.

59   HRO, 148M71/2/7/4.

government in 1577 also shows that there were then three inns in the town.[60] Another in 1622 lists five.[61] Physically, inns could be distinguished from large merchant houses by the provision of substantial numbers of individual rooms, although it should be noted that such private rooms could each provide for several people with more than one bed and more than one person per bed. Such proliferation of rooms can be seen in the inventories of innkeepers, as in those of Jane Cowslade in 1592, John Buckler in 1625, and John Crosse in 1625, where between seven and ten separate chambers were provided in each inn.[62] The absence of earlier evidence reflects the destruction of buildings and documentation in the succeeding centuries.[63] We have little evidence of inn names and these may have changed but in 1542 a rental records The Angel, The Swan and The George, to which should be added The Hart Inn in 1474, The Bell probably in 1513 and 1622, The Crown in 1535, The Chequer in 1560 and 1622, and The Maidenhead in 1622.[64] Two names were longstanding. The George was found in 1442, 1518 and 1622, and again in 1762 (Fig. 15).[65] The Angel remained here in 1560, 1622 and until after 1850.[66] Only occasionally can inn and innkeeper be linked. Thomas Pette (Pytte) was innkeeper in 1531–58, but is described specifically as keeping the Swan Inn in 1535.[67] The George, in 1542, was held by a Kent, probably Richard in 1534 and 1544/5. The inns were probably concentrated in the upper part of town on the main road between Winchester and London and in the market place.

In Basingstoke, as elsewhere, innkeepers were part of a wealthy urban elite.[68] They played an important marketing role for food, not merely for bread and ale. In 1519 and 1520, the court accused the innkeepers of taking up all the fresh fish, keeping the best and selling what was left at an excessive price to the poor: 'Then as we might have of the fisher five herrings for a penny, they will sell us but four herrings for a penny'.[69] In 1420, inn-holders were forbidden to buy fish before the bailiff had seen it and set it on sale.[70]

The innkeeper was frequently rich and powerful figures within the community, and often came from well-established family. A good early example of this may be seen in the career of Richard Kingsmill who was Basingstoke's leading innkeeper from 1454 to 1470. He sold bread and horsebread, and was fined 10s. as a hostiller in 1454 (compared

60   TNA, SP 12/2117/74.
61   HRO, 44M69/G3/166.
62   HRO, 1592A/031; 1625AD/020; 1625AD/034. No doubt at least one of these rooms would have been for the innkeeper himself.
63   For discussion of the physical and documentary evidence elsewhere in Hampshire see J. Hare, 'Inns, innkeepers and the society of late medieval England' and Roberts, *Hampshire Houses*, 179–83.
64   Baigent & Millard, *Basingstoke*, 564, 332, 343, 318, 322, 326, 343, 664, 295.
65   HRO, 148M71/2/1/40; Baigent & Millard, *Basingstoke*, 315.
66   Baigent & Millard, *Basingstoke*, 343; HRO, 10M57/E62; 42M66/83; 4A6/6; 10M57/SP132/1; One building contains medieval structures but may represent a later inn (Bill Fergie, 'The former Anchor public house, London Street, Basingstoke', *HFC Newsletter* 58 (2012), 17.
67   HRO, 148M71/2/7/19; 2/1/66, 67; 2/7/21, 22, 27; 34; Baigent & Millard, *Basingstoke*, 326. The dates of innkeeping have been based on the surviving lists of fines, most of which were examined and may be incomplete.
68   For a general treatment of innkeepers see J. Hare, 'Inns, innkeepers and the society of late medieval England', 191–2; and A. Everitt, 'The English urban inn 1560–1760', in A. Everitt (ed.), *Perspectives on English Urban History, 1350–1600* (1973), 91–137.
69   Baigent & Millard, *Basingstoke*, 323.
70   Baigent & Millard, *Basingstoke*, 323, and see also 324–5.

Figure 14 *Building within the former Angel Inn, Winchester Street, demolished c.1960. This large building and its elaborate painting, reflect the prosperity of the inn-keeping industry in the 16th century.*

with only 6*s*. 8*d*. for the two other innkeepers) and an additional 1*s*. fine for brewing. In 1470 he was fined 12*s*., again appreciably more than the other two innkeepers and much more than the fines of those with other occupations.[71] He was a rich townsman, with the highest assessment for the subsidy of 1481, and his rent payment in 1480–3 was about twice the next highest payment, and he had leased the hospital of St John from Merton College from 1455 to 1466.[72] He was active in local government serving as royal constable in 1455, as town bailiff in 1464–5 and 1487–8, as well as J.P., M.P. and tax assessor.[73] He marketed cloth in 1467 but his interests went far beyond the urban world of Basingstoke. In 1462–3 he imported goods direct from Southampton: wine, fish and fruit.[74] He bought land in a small neighbouring town of Whitchurch in 1470, was described as grazier, yeoman and gentleman, possessed substantial sheep flocks of over 200 wethers, and leased a nearby demesne at Ashe.[75] He could act as proctor for Mapledurwell, one of the

71   HRO, 148M71/2/7/4 & 7.
72   HRO, 148M71/3/4/1; Baigent & Millard, *Basingstoke*, 380–1, 615–16.
73   J.C. Wedgwood, *History of Parliament: Biographies of Members of the Commons House 1439–1509* (London: H.M.S.O., 1936), 516–17; *ODNB*, s.v. 'Kingsmill Family (*c.*1480–1698)', gentry (accessed Jan. 2017).
74   TNA, E 101/344/17, m. 18; *Overland Trade Database*.
75   HRO, 19M61/2.

neighbouring villages in its dispute with its rector.[76] The family were already well-established in the town, with William Kingsmill having been bailiff in 1390–1.

The wealth and influential role of innkeepers in the town is seen both among his predecessors and successors. The atte Welles provide one example. Philip was an attorney in 1440 and mercer in 1448,[77] John was an innkeeper in 1454–78, while Christian atte Welle was involved in the related task of importing wine from Southampton in 1462 and 1463, and was a miller in 1478.[78] John Clerke was an innkeeper in 1484–91, but had other substantial financial activities. He leased the rectory from 1496/7 to 1504/5, he brewed in 1490 and 1497, was described as husbandman, and left £2 to repairs to the church in his will of 1505.[79] Later John Hopkyns, innkeeper from 1546 to 1581, was one of the richest men in town in the 1559 tax assessment, and was alderman of the Guild of the Holy Ghost in 1566. He also acted as a Royal Postmaster in 1579, dispatching royal packages and hiring out horses and post boys.[80] Romblow Wadelow, innkeeper (1585) was one of the most highly assessed in the 1586 subsidy, with only two others assessed above him.[81] George Yate, innkeeper in 1584 and 1590, was less highly assessed in the 1586 subsidy, but was bailiff in 1584 and 1590. He was another innkeeper who acted as a Royal Postmaster, with responsibility for delivering royal packages from Basingstoke, in his case between 1595 and 1601.[82] Some men like John Belchamber were actively involved in the cloth industry while others merely benefitted from the general prosperity that it produced. William Lancaster was innkeeper from 1558 to 1583. He came from a family well-established in the town and cloth industry in the early 16th century, with Richard, Hugh and the latter's son James all being drapers.[83] James' London connections are reflected in being able to place two of his sons as apprentices to London merchants, for one of whom this was the opening to international activities and success.[84]

The subsidies of 1523/5 allow us to place the innkeepers within the town's structure of wealth.[85] At least, three of the four assessed innkeepers of 1524, were part of the rich urban elite, with wealth and frequent longstanding role within the town. John Belchamber was the richest of the innkeepers in 1523 and one of the wealthiest men in the town, being assessed at the highest figure of £80. Like Kingsmill, his family was a well-established part of the urban elite. William was a miller in 1448, and Joanna was in

76   Corpus Christi College, Oxford, Muniments C 6 cap. 13 (1), 2 (I am grateful to Dr Jean Morrin for this reference).

77   Baigent & Millard, *Basingstoke*, 269; HRO, 148M71/2/7/4–2/7/8.

78   HRO, 148M71 2/7/3, 4, 5, 7; *Brokage Books database*. It is not clear whether there was any link between this family and the atte Welle innkeepers of the nearby town of Alresford, where Philip atte Welle was an innkeeper in 1436 until shortly before the inn burnt down in 1439/40, and John in period after its rebuilding in 1461 WCM, 1840–56.

79   Mag. Coll., 56/ 15–7.

80   HRO, 148M71/ 2/7/27, 34, 35, 2/1/82; Baigent & Millard, *Basingstoke*, 398, 128; M. Brayshay. 'The royal pack-horse routes of Hampshire in the reign of Elizabeth I', *PHFC* 48 (1992), 123, 133.

81   HRO, 148M71/2/1/92; 1586; *Hants Lay Subsidy Rolls, 1586*, 39–40.

82   HRO, 148M72/1/ 90, 92; *Hants Lay Subsidy Rolls, 1586*, 39–40. A Thomas Yates, presumably a relation, was then assessed on possession of land: Baigent & Millard, *Basingstoke*, 438; HRO, 148M71 /2/7/35; Brayshay, 'The royal pack-horse routes of Hampshire', 133.

83   HRO, 148M71/2/7/16; 18; 27.

84   M. Franks, *The Basingstoke Admiral: a life of Sir James Lancaster* (2006), 3, 177–84, 222–4.

85   HRO, 148M71/3/4/2.

court in 1464.[86] Another John, probably his father, was a leading figure until his death in 1513 as bailiff, tenant, fishmonger and mercer, possessor of a fulling mill and his will revealed him as both a generous benefactor to the church and with an income from the Bell (see above, p. 60). John Belchamber, the innkeeper, was previously a mercer in 1515–16, engaging in the import of high quality imported cloth and luxuries and the export of woollen cloth and one of a small rich group of traders in the town. He was documented as an innkeeper in 1524, and fined as a merchant or mercer and fishmonger from 1530 to 1540. He was recorded as a tenant in 1524 and 1541–2.[87] He was a church warden in 1517, bailiff three times in 1516, 1535 and 1539, and a high collector of the subsidy in Basingstoke hundred in the 1520s. After his death (in 1542), he was described as a clothier, but had already migrated out of town and returned to the neighbouring village of Cliddesden, where his descendants remained in the 17th century. John was part of an urban elite and was executor to another rich innkeeper, John Couslade.[88] Thomas Lane, a rich mercer of the town, described John Belchamber in his will as 'my brother' (probably brother-in-law).[89] Of the other innkeepers in 1524 John Couslade, was assessed highly (45*s*.), imported wine directly from Southampton in 1527–8, and held land in the nearby towns of Kingsclere and Hungerford as well as in Basingstoke. He left the large sum of £20 to his son.[90] Elizabeth Deane (20*s*.) was probably the widow of one of the richest men in town.

The records give the impression that innkeeping was a largely male preserve, although this may produce a distorted view of a situation in which women might be just as active and involved as men. Here, as in so many different walks of life, widowhood gave women a chance to achieve legal independence as with Margery Pottinger (innkeeper 1498–1516) or Rachel Wadlow (1585).[91] The inn might also be passed on from father or widow to son. A good example of this family pattern is provided by the Cowslade family, who were active in the town from the early 15th century. As we have seen, John was innkeeper from 1516 to 1536. He was succeeded by his wife Joanna who was innkeeper in 1536–44, followed by James Cowslade in 1552–71, and by his widow Jane in 1581 and 1582.[92] The Kents were another family of innkeepers. John was fined from 1499 until his death in 1523.[93] Later a Richard was an innkeeper from 1530–39, and so was another John briefly in 1540.[94]

86   HRO, 148M71/2/1/46; 2/1/47
87   HRO, 148M71/2/7/18; Baigent & Millard, *Basingstoke*, 319, HRO, 148M71/2/7/18, 19; 22; 3/1/10 & 11.
88   HRO, 1536B/13.
89   HRO, 1536B/13.
90   *Overland Trade Database*; HRO, 1536 B/13.
91   HRO, 148M71/2/7/2, 16, 65, 17; 2/1/92.
92   HRO, 148M71/2/7/21, 22, 24, 27; 2/7/30–35; 2/7/34. Some of the gaps would no doubt be filled by further documentation.
93   HRO, 148M71/2/7/12, 2/1/65; 1523B/20. He had borrowed £11 in London in 1497: J. Mackman and M. Stevens, *Court of Common Pleas: the National Archives, CP40 1399–1500* (London, 2010), *British History Online*: http://www.british-history.ac.uk/no-series/common-pleas/1399-1500 (accessed 28 Jan. 2017). [TNA, CP 40/951, rot. 343].
94   HRO, 148M71/2/7/19, 2/7/21; 2/7/22.

Social Life

Regulation and Order

The activities of the courts provide insights into urban life, but they focus on when things went wrong and do not therefore provide a typical view of life at the time any more than now.[95] Essentially the hundred court and the court of frankpledge, offered a gathering where the townsmen could get together to deal with offences and decide what was necessary to ensure the smooth running of the town. Assaults were an obvious matter to be dealt with. As ever some may have been pre-planned and others not, as suggested by some of the weapons employed: a candle stick or a card for carding wool.[96] There were cases involving the regulations of agriculture (see above, pp. 28–9) such as overstocking the pastures, ploughing beyond one's own strips or failing to maintain the hedges and ditches. There were cases involving the maintenance of the urban substructure: blocking or neglect of roads or bridges, or the maintenance of the motte hall, or on the eve of the Armada in 1587, to improve the Butts.[97] There were cases of debt, whose management was essential to the running of the local economy. Other cases also dealt with what were perceived to be anti-social activities. Manufacturing sometime led to anti-social actions. Dyeing cloth and the washing and preparing of leather used much water and produced unpleasant effluent. Emptying dyeing vats into the river could not take place before 9 p.m. or after 9 a.m.[98] On one occasion, the infringement was evident, the dyers emptying the vat between 12 p.m. and 2 p.m.[99] Glovers were found washing skins in the common river and reminded that this was not to be done after 6 p.m.[100] One glover, John Normanton in 1587, threw the water onto the road outside, and had evidently done this several times.[101] Much required a balance of interests: the vicar might think it a good idea to erect a privy over the common brook, but it 'is a great nuisance to all, those who washed there' and he was ordered to remove it.[102]

We know little of the social entertainment, but occasionally the courts hint at some of the ways in which time was passed and which seemed to involve social dangers: drinking, gambling and cards, and inappropriate arms. As we have seen already (see p. 38) ale, and then beer, flavoured with hops, were an important part of life and diet. Ale sellers needed to mark their house with an appropriate ale pole, to keep good rule, and hours were regulated.[103] In 1515 the regulations distinguished between apprentices, who could only remain until 7 p.m. while servants could remain until 9 p.m.[104] The latter time seems already to have represented closing time in the early 15th century, as

95   On the work of the courts see the extracts in Baigent & Millard, *Basingstoke*, 240–356.
96   Baigent & Millard, *Basingstoke*, 286, 257.
97   Baigent & Millard, *Basingstoke*, 308, 311–15, 342, 351.
98   Baigent & Millard, *Basingstoke*, 310: here the finishing time was earlier (3 p.m.).
99   Baigent & Millard, *Basingstoke*, 310, 343.
100 Baigent & Millard, *Basingstoke*, 349.
101 Baigent & Millard, *Basingstoke*, 352, 353.
102 Baigent & Millard, *Basingstoke*, 337.
103 Baigent & Millard, *Basingstoke*, 335.
104 Baigent & Millard, *Basingstoke*, 320.

in 1425 and 1440, although in 1442 one man was indicted as a player of dice and hazard by day and night, and in 1510 the offence was playing cards rather than the timing.[105] In 1518, it was decided that householders, journeymen and apprentices should not wear knives and daggers on Sundays and holydays[106] (when, no doubt, crowds gathered and people had time on their hands). The growth of town and cloth industry may have made the issue of controlling a larger proletariat more of a problem. There was some sort of night regulation or night watchers, while two men were accused of being common night wanderers with bows and swords.[107]

Educating the Young

Evidence about education is frustratingly fragmentary. Nevertheless, it is clear that at least some of the citizens and tradesmen of the town valued education and were prepared to invest in this for their sons' future. John Grene in 1583 left a bequest for the son of a cousin to be kept at school.[108] By the 15th century, the limited education would have been provided by chantry priests, although there is no specific evidence for Basingstoke. By the time the chantries were closed in 1547–8 under Edward VI, the Holy Ghost chapel had taken on such responsibilities. The guild there, whose purpose had originally been to provide a priest, had shifted to providing a school master.[109] This may have represented a formalisation of an informal function, or a means of justifying the continuation of the guild in a changing religious context. The educational role was emphasised when under Queen Mary the townsmen were able to restore the Holy Ghost guild and its land.[110] Then, under Queen Elizabeth, the guild was refounded and continued with its educational aim, appointing a school master in 1559.[111] This shift in emphasis was reflected in the wardens being referred to, from 1569 to 1577, as wardens of the Holy Ghost School.[112] The shift from priest and chantries to education meant that the school master became an urban institution. Now some of the wills recorded bequests to the schoolmaster.[113]

Some Basingstoke boys were educated outside the town. One opportunity lay within the church although this can rarely be quantified. However, a thorough study has been made of the personnel of the county's greatest and richest monastery, that of the cathedral priory at Winchester from the 13th century onwards. The monks usually took the name of their place of origin and these toponymics suggest the importance of Basingstoke. It suggests that Basing and Basingstoke, although they produced marginally fewer recruits than Winchester, were, after the cathedral city, by far and away the most common source for monks.[114] This reflects both the importance of the town and the

---

105 Baigent & Millard, *Basingstoke*, 258, 272, 280, 310.
106 Baigent & Millard, *Basingstoke*, 322.
107 Baigent & Millard, *Basingstoke*, 279, 325, 336, 276.
108 HRO, 28M49/1.
109 Baigent & Millard, *Basingstoke*, 663.
110 Baigent & Millard, *Basingstoke*, 125–6, 663–7.
111 Baigent & Millard, *Basingstoke*, 137; for subsequent school masters in this period see 138–43.
112 Millard, *Holy Ghost*, 29–40.
113 e.g. HRO, 1587/B/82; 28M49; 148M71/8/5/2 or 5M52/U.
114 J. Greatrex, *Biographical Register of the English Cathedral Priories of the Province of Canterbury, c.1066–1540* (Oxford, 1997), 636, 668–722, 748–53.

attitudes of some of its inhabitants. The last prior and first Dean of the cathedral was himself a Basingstoke man, from a well-known family, the Kingsmills. Just before the Dissolution, his mother Alice Tetrydge of Basingstoke, a widow, was granted a lease of the manor and manor house of Silkstead.[115]

The development of schools and linked colleges in the later Middle Ages also opened up new opportunities. Winchester College provided one such opening. Between 1395 and 1537, at least 21 boys went from Basingstoke to Winchester College.[116] Between 1395 and 1450 there were four, between 1450 and 1499 five; and between 1500 and 1537 there were twelve. It tended to be the better-off who were recruited as reflected by the tax assessment of 1523 (see above, pp. 57–8). If we examine the 12 who went to Winchester College between 1500 and 1537, five came from the richest families, three from the middling sort and two were assessed at the standard rate, with another two unknown. The pattern was already evident earlier. Thus John Cook, who went to the college in 1471, was probably son of Edward Cook, a mercer with the second highest assessment on goods in the 1481 subsidy assessment.[117]

Some can be tracked after they went to the college and some evidently achieved considerable success outside Basingstoke. One obvious example was John Kingsmill, the son of Richard the leading innkeeper and prominent citizen of the town. John went to New College Oxford and after a successful academic start, was an earlier pioneer in the shift from a university career to the common law which was such an important feature of the 16th century. He ended up in the exalted national position as a justice of the Common Pleas.[118] Robert Sherborne was described as both of Sherborne and of Basingstoke and may have belonged to the country gentry, but ended up as a bishop and high government official.[119] Thomas Greenway, who went to the college in 1533, achieved mixed success in Oxford University and the church. From Winchester he went to Corpus Christi College, Oxford (1537), became Fellow of the College in 1541, and a canon of Christ Church (in 1554) and President of Corpus Christi College (1562–8). In a critical visitation by the protestant Bishop Horne of Winchester in 1566, he was accused of a variety of offences. The underlying cause of the attacks may have been religious, and from his reluctance to espouse protestant views, but they focussed on attacks on his lifestyle (his eight mistresses, his drunkenness, attendance at bull-baiting and bear-baiting), and on financial irregularities (taking money for himself that, it was claimed, should have gone to the college), and on the benefit he gave to members of his family. He

---

115 Greatrex, *Biographical Register*, 672. Tetrydge was a tailor with a mid-ranking assessment in 1523.

116 I am grateful to Dr Rebecca Oakes for providing a list of students from Basingstoke, including both those described as from Basingstoke in the Winchester College records, and four whose place of origin is recorded only in the New College archives.

117 Baigent & Millard, *Basingstoke*, 395.

118 Emden, *OU Reg. to 1500* II, 1074–5; R.L. Storey, 'The foundation of the medieval College, 1379–1530', in J. Buxton and P. Williams, *New College Oxford, 1379–1979* (1979), 36; *ODNB*, s.v. Kingsmill family (*per. c.*1480–1698), gentry (accessed 10 Jan. 2017).

119 Emden, *OU Reg. to 1500* III, 1685; *ODNB*, s.v. Sherborn [Sherborne], Robert (*c.*1454–1536), bishop of Chichester (accessed 17 Jan. 2017).

spent the rest of his life at his rectories and was a generous benefactor to the college; its library still contains 63 of his volumes.[120]

How far the family in Basingstoke benefitted is unclear. Certainly John Greenway acquired land from the college, and three Greenways gained studentships or scholarships at the college immediately after his tenure as President.[121] John Potynger went to New College and becoming a fellow there. He returned to Winchester College as an usher, which he left on his marriage and ended up as a schoolmaster teaching grammar to the young monks, and to the boys of the almonry and the chapel at the Cathedral Priory.[122]

The three sons of William Lancaster all went to Corpus Christi College, Oxford, although possibly after he had left Basingstoke through education.[123]

But most of the Basingstoke recruits to Winchester College did not take the academic route and left no trace in Oxford. They may have returned to careers in Basingstoke but only rarely can this be established. John Belchamber, who entered the college in 1490, was the son of another John Belchamber who had died a rich man in 1513 after a career as a mercer, fishmonger and bailiff. His son was to receive a fulling mill, a sixth of his father's goods and a prestigious house in the market place.[124] The opportunities were great and he, in turn, became a rich and powerful member of the community (see above, pp. 69–70). Another returner might be John Cooke. He went to Winchester College (1471) and New College (1479) becoming a fellow in 1481 before vacating this position in 1484 and apparently disappearing from Oxford.[125] His likely father, Edward, had died in 1495, but was followed in Basingstoke by a John, who was probably our student, and who died in 1517, leaving two sons, John and Edward.[126]

But there were other educational institutions, apart from Winchester College, to which some of the citizens might turn. Thomas Canner recorded in a letter to Thomas Cromwell that Basingstoke was the place of his birth, and the family is known both in Basingstoke and in neighbouring Mapledurwell, but he had already established an importance beyond these places.[127] He went to Magdalen College Oxford (possibly via its associated school) and this became the start of a successful career in Oxford and the church. He was a fellow and holder of various offices at Magdalen, moving on to Cardinal Wolsey's new foundation of Cardinal (later Christ Church) College in Oxford. He held various rectories and was archdeacon of Dorset

---

120 Emden, *OU Reg. 1501–1540*, 245; *Alumni Oxoniensis* II, 600; J. McConnica (ed.), *The History of the University of Oxford, III, The Collegiate University* (Oxford 1986), 17, 408, 409, 459, 462; *Reg. Horne*, HRO, 21M65/A1/26; He was probably the brother of John Greenway the elder who died in 1576, although this was after Thomas' death so that there is no mention of the relationship in the will (TNA, PROB 11/60/180).

121 *Alumni Oxoniensis* II, 600.

122 Emden, *OU Reg.* 1501–40, 459.

123 J.K. McConica and C.S. Knighton, 'Some 16th century Corpus families: Kingsmills, Nappers, Lancaster & others', *The Pelican* (1978–9), 8.

124 HRO, 1513B/1; 148M71; 2/7/12; 2/1/65.

125 Emden, *OU Reg. to 1500*, 455.

126 HRO, 1495B/1; 1517B/8.

127 *L & P Hen. VIII*, IV(2), 1695; *Mapledurwell*, 50–1. The family was recorded in the town from 1425 (Baigent & Millard, *Basingstoke*, 258).

before his death by 1551.[128] John Delacourt was admitted to Magdalen College in 1491 and was a fellow there from at least 1498 to 1510. He came from the Winchester diocese but the unusual surname suggests a link with the Basingstoke fuller from 1478.[129]

Others found a career through training in the law. John Couslade, another wealthy innkeeper and member of a well-established family in the town, left money to his son Robert for three years as long as he continued learning at an Inn of Chancery.[130]

Apprenticeships were another form of training and advancement, whereby parents used their contacts and their capital to enable a son to be apprenticed to a career. The town's good contacts with London merchants enabled many to join the influx of provincial youth who flocked to the capital and enabled its population to expand so fast. It is difficult to document this process, but a few examples can show this in operation, James Lancaster apprenticed two of his sons to different members of the skinners company in London: James in 1571 and Peter in 1576.[131] James Dean was apprenticed to a London draper and ended up as the Master of the Drapers' company, a city alderman, and a major benefactor to Basingstoke.[132] Richard Puckeridge was apprenticed to a haberdasher and his father left him a legacy to be paid through a London haberdasher, his master.[133] Nearer to hand, some were settled in Southampton and established themselves as merchants there, often trading with their parental town, as with William Grete and Robert Ronanger.[134]

Looking After the People: Charity

The hospital of St John provided support for elderly clergy and the poor (see below). It was expected to provide for a chaplain, a clerk and two poor people, although this was not always done.[135] This also provided for a system of corrodies where, in return for cash, a few elderly people were looked after in their old age. Some citizens left money for the poor after their death or burial.[136] An almshouse existed in the middle of the 16th century. It is recorded in a rental of 1541–2 and Elizabeth West made a small payment to the almshouse in Basingstoke in 1543.[137] Moreover, just outside our period came the foundation of the almshouse that still survives today: that founded by Sir James Deane in London Street in 1607.[138] One will shows evidence of wider provision for the poor. Thomas Brown was the vicar of Basingstoke and Kingsclere until his death in 1588. His bequests to the poor included references to the existence

---

128 Emden, *OU Reg. 1501–40*, 98–9.

129 Emden, *OU Reg. to 1500*, 357–8; HRO, 148M71/2/7/8; 2/7/16.

130 HRO, 1536B/13.

131 Franks, *Basingstoke Admiral*, 15, 19.

132 On the London Lancasters and Deans see above, 50.

133 HRO, 1574B/136.

134 J. Hare, 'Small towns', 96–7; T.B. James, *The geographical origins and mobility of the inhabitants of Southampton, 1400–1600* (unpublished Ph.D. thesis, University of St Andrews, 1977), 132, 495.

135 Baigent & Millard, *Basingstoke*, 50–1.

136 e.g. HRO, 1536B/13, 1544B/110, 1570B/1/56; TNA, PROB 11/88/350, PROB 11/75/41.

137 Baigent & Millard, *Basingstoke*, 385–6; HRO, 1543U/18.

138 Baigent & Millard, *Basingstoke*, 708–9; HRO, 5M52/C1; 148M71/8/5/2.

of a poor men's box at Basingstoke, Kingsclere, Basing, Odiham, Alton, Newbury, Combe and Nutley. This was in addition to payments to the poor of Basingtoke, Kingsclere, Echinswell and Sydmonton. He also left money for two scholarships to Oxford, from Kingsclere and Basingstoke, and money to be lent to the poorer sort of clothiers. These were probably men who were starting up business on their own.[139]

139 HRO, 1588B/9.

Parochial Organisation

BASINGSTOKE BEGAN AS a chapel belonging to a much larger parish which was dependent on the mother church of Basing, a village outside the main town. This break up of a large area dependent on a mother church was a common development in the Wessex area, as individual lords created a series of smaller private units or parishes. In Hampshire, such large ecclesiastical units had remained normal until the 11th century, but there was a proliferation of churches catering for new small parishes in the 12th century.[1] By the end of that century, changes in canon law made it much more difficult to create new parishes. This restrictive approach seems to have been more fully applied after the accession to the bishopric of Winchester in 1172 of Richard of Ilchester with his more legalistic approach. Subsequently the creation of new parishes virtually ceased.[2] Although the creation of new smaller units had reduced the area dependent on the mother church, Basing remained an exceptionally large parish which included Basing itself and the chapels of Basingstoke and Up Nately. The situation in this parish was further complicated by the growth of the town of Basingstoke which soon became economically much more important than the original mother settlement. Basing and Basingstoke remained part of a single parochial unit until 1864.[3]

The advowson of Basing, with its church and chapels, had been granted to the Norman monastery of Mont Saint Michel, and was in its possession by 1086, in Domesday Book, when Basing church possessed a priest, two villeins, four bordars, a hide of land, a mill and a meadow.[4] Subsequently, Peter des Roches, bishop of Winchester, bought the church and estate in order to provide part of the endowment of his new foundation of Selborne Priory, a nearby house of Augustinian canons which he founded in 1233/4.[5] Basing and Basingstoke remained with Selborne until the latter's dissolution in 1485, when Bishop William Waynflete used its income to endow his new foundation of Magdalen College, Oxford.[6] From 1233/4, the financial benefits of the rectory and the choice of vicar went to Selborne, and subsequently Magdalen College, but they were required to use part of the income and tithes to provide a vicar for the

1   P.H. Hase, 'The mother churches of Hampshire', in J. Blair (ed.), *Ministers and Parish Churches: the Local Churches in transition, 950–1200* (Oxford, 1988), 51.
2   P.H. Hase, 'The church in the Wessex heartlands', in M. Aston and C. Lewis (eds), *The Medieval Landscape of Wessex* (Oxford, 1994), 62–72.
3   Baigent & Millard, *Basingstoke*, 27–8.
4   *Domesday*, 101; Confirmation in 1194, Macray, *Selborne* I, 1; M.J. Franklin (ed.), *English Episcopal Acta, Winchester, 1070–1204* (Oxford, 1993), 171–2.
5   Macray, *Selborne* I, 9–10; II, 3–4; *Cal. Chart.* I, 182–3.
6   Macray, *Selborne* I, 119–45.

combined parish. It was thus the vicar, rather than the rector, who was the key religious figure in the town, and who was himself endowed by particular tithes.[7]

One interesting feature that emerges from the documentation for Basing and Basingstoke is the changing balance between the mother and daughter churches, which resulted from the growing economic importance of Basingstoke. In the 1190s and at the beginning of the 13th century the documentation refers to Basing (and sometimes to its dependent chapels).[8] When setting up Selborne priory in 1233–4, the documents refer to the churches of Basing and Basingstoke, as if they were equals.[9] A few years later, by 1244, when establishing or regulating the vicarage, precedence was given to Basingstoke, the subordinate upstart. The vicar was referred to as serving the churches of Basingstoke and Basing, and the chapel of Nately, but the vicar was to live in Basingstoke with two chaplains and was to provide two chaplains in Basing.[10] The town's precedence remained thereafter. Basing was now steadily referred to as a chapel of Basingstoke, and the last reference so far located to a dual parish was in 1294.[11] It was only in 1864 that Basing itself became an independent parish.[12] The vicars can be listed,[13] but it is perhaps more revealing to focus on one particularly well-documented example, that of Richard Gosmer. Richard had a career at Magdalen College before being granted the vicarage which itself lay in its patronage. He was a fellow of the college from 1489 to 1499, third and then second bursar, and supervisor for the building of the new tower there (1495–7), before becoming vice president and then being granted Basingstoke in 1499. He remained in the town until 1541, when he retired to his other rectory at Ewhurst (Surrey) until his death in 1547.[14] He was active in the life of the town, as shown in contemporary wills, where he was usually one of the witnesses, probably in the rebuilding of the parish church, and in the remarkable evidence of the financial notes he recorded in a volume. The latter indicate some of the range of his activity within the parish: the collection of tithes, disputes about them, and sale of the tithes within the community, whether to a wealthy local merchant or an alewife; borrowing, lending and employing; his responsibilities as vicar whether looking after the church service books, the vicarage buildings, recording a contract between two traders, or as a witness for wills. They can both hint at the vicar and his relations with his parish community, and in incidental references can shed light on the workings of the local economy and community.[15] Gosmer was very much part of

---

7   Macray, *Selborne* II, 9–10, 16–8.

8   Macray, *Selborne* II, 1–2.

9   Macray, *Selborne* II, 3, 4, 5; I, 10, 9, 14, 11; N. Vincent, *English Episcopal Acta* IX, *Winchester* 1205–1238 (Oxford, 1994), 39, 41, 42.

10   Macray, *Selborne* II, 17.

11   P.H. Hase, *The Development of the Parish in Hampshire particularly in the Eleventh and Twelfth Centuries* (unpublished Ph.D. thesis, Univ. of Cambridge, 1975), 316.

12   Baigent & Millard, *Basingstoke*, 27–8.

13   For lists up to 1499 see D.G. Le Faye, 'Selborne Priory and the vicarage of Basingstoke', *PHFC* 46 (1990), 97–8; for 1499–1864 see Baigent & Millard, *Basingstoke*, 22–8.

14   Emden, *OU Reg. to 1500* II, 794.

15   C.U.L., MS Ll.2.2. See R.N. Swanson, 'Profits, priests and people', in C. Burgess and E. Duffy, *The Parish in Late Medieval England*, Harlaxton Medieval Studies XIV (Donington, 2006), 157–9; and his, 'A universal levy: tithes and economic agency', in B. Dodds and R. Britnell (eds), *Agriculture and Rural Society after the Black Death* (Hertford, 2008), 99, 102.

the local community, aided by a small group of curates and chaplains (four in 1520, serving Basingstoke, Basing and Up Nately).[16] As vicar, he did not receive the income from the rectory, but he leased this from Magdalen College in 1501–17.[17]

The Parish Church of St Michael

Basingstoke's parish church is one of the finest late medieval churches in Hampshire and was completely rebuilt in the 15th and early 16th centuries. It provides a fitting tribute to the town's economic prosperity. The church consists of a small chancel and a much larger nave and aisles. The chapel, south of the chancel is medieval, but that to the north was added in 1920 as a memorial to the dead of the First World War. The church has a large tower at its west end and a south porch with chamber above (Figs 16 & 17). The eastern part of the church provides the earliest surviving part of the building, and is constructed of flint with stone dressings as was typical of the medieval churches of Hampshire, where ashlar was not easily accessible.[18]

We know nothing of the original church but by the 13th century, this had become a large aisled structure, since the new, and still surviving, 14th-century chapel south of the chancel pre-supposes the existence of both the chancel to the north and an aisle, or at least a transept to the west. It also incorporates some earlier reused ashlar mixed with the flint. The church was evidently already on a larger scale than the village churches around, apart from the mother church of Basing itself. It also grew before the great rebuilding of the later 15th and early 16th centuries. The south-east chapel has already been noted. The wide aisles are of very different construction suggesting that the northern one may have represented an earlier widening, whose shell was then reused and re-fenestrated when the southern aisle was widened and rebuilt in ashlar in the later 15th century. Traditionally, church buildings in this area used the locally-available material, whether flint or the soft greensand or malmstone, as in the chancel and probably originally in the nave. The wall of the north aisle seems to have followed this pattern, appearing from the interior to be rubble covered with plaster, while externally, the chequerboard of flint and ashlar represents a later re-facing of the rubble wall, replacing earlier mortar covering, and which had been put in place by the early 19th century.[19] By contrast the new wider south aisle was constructed of the more expensive squared ashlar. Finally, the tower's lower windows would stylistically seem to date to the late 14th- or early 15th-century.

The maintenance of the chancel was the responsibility of the rector, then Selborne Priory, who rebuilt the chancel in c.1462–5. A payment in the priory records in 1464–5 refers to the 'new building of the chancel of Basyngstoke church', and to a further payment of £70 'parcel of the £120 of the first contract for building the said chancel of Basingstoke'.[20] A payment of such a large sum would have been a considerable investment for a poor priory like Selborne, which received an annual rent of £20 from the rectory at

16   HRO, 21M65 B1/1 f.43r.
17   Mag. Coll., 57/16; EL/2 n2.
18   NHL, no. 1092618, Church of St Michael (accessed 8 Feb. 2017).
19   Noted in an account of about 1815 (HRO, 29M51/7/3) and in Sir Stephen Glynne's account in 1839–40 (my thanks to Barry Meehan for this reference).
20   Mag. Coll., Selborne 381; Macray, *Selborne* I, 114–15.

Figure 16 *Church of St Michael from SE, showing the much larger scale of the parishioners' new nave and aisles, late 15th and early 16th centuries, compared with the earlier eastern arm on the right hand side (2017).*

the turn of the century, and possessed a potential total 15th-century income of between about £50 and £70.[21] Since this was being done at the same time as other works by the priory, it seems likely that this represented investment by Bishop Waynflete who intended to use Selborne to endow his new college, and would have wished to avoid a future drain on Magdalen's resources that might arise from the need for major repairs. The chancel was not rebuilt from the foundations. In all probability, the walls were kept, but new windows and a new roof were added together with now lost fittings. The fine roof survives fully, and stylistically it would fit with the documented date (Fig. 18).[22] Later, in 1528, a new doorway into the chancel was added and this still survives. The east window is not original, but replaced that damaged by bombing during the Second World War.

The nave was the responsibility of the parishioners and they completely rebuilt it on a much grander scale in the later 15th and early 16th centuries. This contrast between chancel and nave is often found in the rebuilding work of wealthy communities in the later Middle Ages, both in rural and urban churches (as with St Thomas' Church, Salisbury, the main church of the great provincial capital).[23] Here, at Basingstoke, a new wide south aisle was built in ashlar, rather than the flint previously used, with large

21   Mag. Coll., 56/15, 16, 24, 25; V. Davis, *William Waynflete: Bishop and educationalist* (Woodbridge, 1993), 148, 157–8.

22   Edward Roberts, pers. comm.

23   T. Tatton-Brown, 'The church of St Thomas of Canterbury, Salisbury', *Wilts. Archaeol. Mag.* 90 (1997), 101–9; Royal Commission on Historic Monuments, *Salisbury* (HMSO, 1980), 24–31.

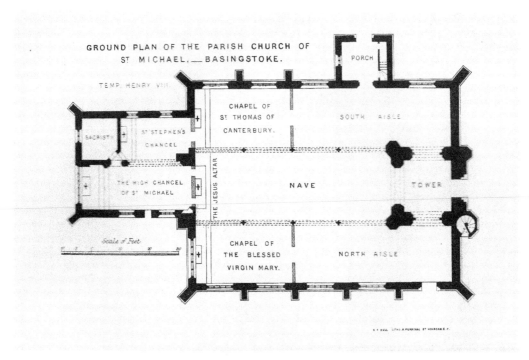

Figure 17 *Plan of St Michael's church. This does not show the NE chapel built after the First World War as a war memorial. (South is at the top.)*

windows such as were also installed in the existing northern aisle. The central portion of the nave was widened and heightened, with its earlier narrower form being still reflected by the narrower dimensions of the tower and the way in which the nave arcade meets it. Basingstoke's nave roof was rebuilt in the 19th century, but it probably re-used earlier material and seems to have incorporated an original design.[24] It would have been a grand roof. Finally, the tower was heightened. It had been begun relatively early in this sequence, judging by the design of its lower windows. It was probably not finished before attention had turned to the much more extensive rebuilding of the nave, but work had probably resumed by 1528 when Thomas Canner petitioned for the bells of the dissolved priory of Wallingford (Berks.) to be given to the church of Basingstoke church, 'where he was brought up'.[25] Another sign that the total scheme was not completed is the high arch at the east end of the south aisle. This would have provided access to a grander replacement for the earlier and lower south chapel (Fig. 16).

The final rebuilding of the clerestory, probably occurred in the generation after 1500 and again uses expensive ashlar. Stylistically, the architectural evidence of the stonework and of the roof implies a late date. The clerestory tracery is very similar to those of the Sandys chapel in the Holy Ghost chapel of the 1520s or 1530s. Moreover, surviving wills suggest the presence of substantial building works in the early 16th century, where money was set aside that was evidently more than the regular token payments for the

24   Baigent & Millard, *Basingstoke*, 88.
25   *L & P Hen VIII*, IV(2), 1526–8, 1, 695.

Figure 18 *Chancel roof, c.1462–5 (2017).*

routine upkeep of the church. John Clerke left 40*s.* in 1505 to the church repairs, John Belchamber left £20 in 1513, Richard Deane £6. 13*s. 4d.* in 1521 and there were smaller payments in 1517, 1522 and two in 1529.[26] The heraldry of the corbels, if original, reinforces an early 16th-century date for the upper levels of the rebuilding, including as they do the arms of Richard Fox, Bishop of Winchester (1501–28). Although the painting is not original, some of the arms, including that of Fox, are cut in relief, and thus indicate the original design.[27]

In conclusion, the rebuilding began with the tower early in the 15th century, followed by the aisles in the second part of the 15th century, at a similar time to the chancel. Rebuilding subsequently resumed or continued with the main part of the nave in the latter part of the 15th century and was finally finished with the clerestory and roof in the first third of the 16th century. The town was then at the peak of its economic importance, and to which the church provides us with a permanent reminder.

Building works continued after Henry VIII's break with Rome. The new porch and room over the porch were under construction in 1540, as shown in three wills of that year, including that of Edward Jenyns who left a small payment 'to the bylding of the Church porche of Basingstoke'.[28] Structurally this is clearly additional to the south aisle. But one obvious sign of religious change was the addition of signs of the royal supremacy over the east end of the nave. When the plaster was being stripped in 1850, paintings

26   Baigent & Millard, *Basingstoke*, 30; HRO, 1513B/1; 1521B/1; 1517B/8; 1522B/14; 1529B/5; 1529B/19.
27   Baigent & Millard, *Basingstoke*, 89–90.
28   HRO, 1540B/35; 1540B/41; 1540B/37.

Figure 19 *Nave of the church and aisles of St Michael, rebuilt in the late 15th and early 16th centuries (2016).*

of a Tudor rose and the feathers of the Prince of Wales were uncovered (as seen in the painting hanging in the north-east chapel), giving us a date between 1537 and 1547, the only time since 1509 when there was a 16th-century Prince of Wales. It thus provides an early example of the impact of Henry's reformation on the inside of a parish church.

The Chapel of the Holy Ghost

Although there was only a single parish church, the importance of the town was reflected in the development of other religious institutions. The chapel of the Holy Ghost, reputedly originated in a graveyard set up outside the town in the interdict of John's reign and in 2017, its ruins overlook the west end of Basingstoke railway station.[29] An alternative explanation of its origin may be that it served a subsidiary settlement on the north side of the Loddon. It was clearly in existence by 1244 when William de Raleigh Bishop of Winchester assigned a third of the offerings to the vicar of Basingstoke, and

---

29   N. Vincent, *Peter des Roches: an alien in English politics, 1205–1238* (Cambridge, 1996), 82, citing VCH *Hants* II, 214, although he adds, 'supposedly founded', 82.

Figure 20 *Exterior of Holy Trinity chapel from the south, showing brick core, ashlar and elaborate decoration (2017).*

it possessed a chaplain by 1250.[30] It soon became a substantial building, able to host the ordination of 140 men in 1309.[31] It was an important element in the late medieval town. Here the major guild of the town was based, dedicated to the Holy Ghost. A list of contributors to the fraternity of the Holy Ghost of Basingstoke survives from *c.*1460.[32] The position of the guild with its alderman, wardens, brothers and sisters, and land holdings, was formalised in a royal charter of 1525.[33] The chapel went through a dramatic rebuilding programme in the early 16th century under the combined efforts of the neighbouring Lord Sandys, of the Vyne, and the citizens themselves. Some work was already underway in 1503, but the main transformation was slightly later.[34] The latter involved both a new chancel east end and a new chantry chapel, the chapel of the Holy Trinity, which Lord Sandys built and where masses would be said for his soul.

Sandys was a leading figure at court who had married a co-heiress of one of Henry VII's leading ministers Sir Reginald Bray and he himself became an important minister in the opening decades of Henry VIII's reign, as a soldier, and treasurer of Calais (1517–26) and then Lord Chamberlain (1527–49).[35] His time in Calais, gave him close

30   Macray, *Selborne* II, 17.
31   Baigent & Millard, *Basingstoke*, 694–6.
32   HRO, 148M71/5/1/1.
33   Baigent & Millard, *Basingstoke*, 118.
34   A. Smith, '"As my lord of Winchester shall devise". Richard Fox and early sixteenth century stained glass in England', *Journal of Stained Glass* 31 (2007), 52.
35   *ODNB*, s.v., Sandys, William, first Baron Sandys (*c.*1470–1540), soldier and courtier (accessed 11 Jan. 2017); M. Howard and E. Wilson, *The Vyne: A Tudor house revealed* (2003), 40–7.

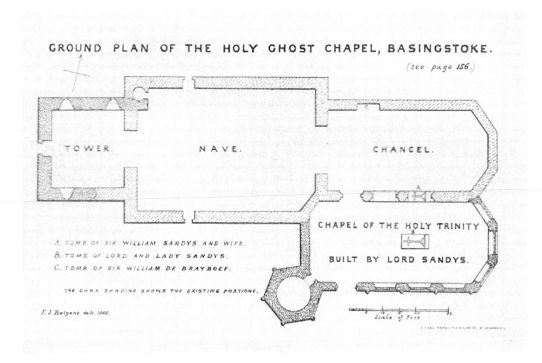

Figure 21 *Plan of Holy Ghost and Holy Trinity chapels.*

*Figure 22
Holy Ghost
chapel
from SE by
Schnebbelie,
c.1800.*

Figure 23 *Queen Margaret of Scotland praying, window in Holy Trinity chapel, now at the Vyne, near Basingstoke. Could the view through the arch of a chapel looking over a town below, with the church and building to its left, represent a memory of the chapel and town as seen during the painters' stay with Sandys in 1522? (See also back cover for enlarged view.)*

continental links, which were reflected in his artistic patronage, and his use of overseas craftsmen for some of the furnishings of the Vyne, a nearby great house which he was rebuilding. But it was also seen in his new chantry chapel here in the magnificent window glass, much of which may still be seen at the Vyne (Fig. 23). He imported glass from Flanders and the windows were in the latest Flemish fashion, probably the work of a group of Flemish glaziers who were employed by Sandys and who stayed with him in 1522.[36] The remarkable sequence of work was noted by contemporaries in the 17th century. It covered the windows in his chapel and those in the chancel of the Holy Ghost chapel, with images representing the life of Christ and of influential contemporary figures or of benefactors, including Henry VIII, his sister Margaret, and Catherine of Aragon. At some point, it was damaged and now 20 per cent of the surviving glass is of Laudian revival date (c.1625–40).[37] It was removed to the Sandys house of the Vyne probably at some time before the siege of Basing house in 1643–5, when lead from the roofs was stripped in order to be melted down and converted into lead shot. It is difficult to imagine careful removal of the glass taking place in such a military context, when the windows also contained much lead.[38] A peacetime removal of windows that were already in decay would also account for the extensive repairs. Sandys' new chapel was not completed until after 1518, when he became a knight of the garter, since his arms on the battlements include the garter, and the glass was not finished until after 1522.[39] Additionally, Sandys commissioned two tombs for the chapel in 1536, one for himself and another for his wife, from an Amsterdam craftsman who was then resident in Artois in north-east France.[40]

Little survives of the main part of the chapel, apart from its ground plan (Fig. 21). But the shell of Sandys' chantry chapel of the Holy Trinity, to the south of the chancel, remains and now prominently overlooks the railway station. The main part of the chapel has a simple plan with a single cell nave, and a chancel. The polygonal east end was probably rebuilt in the early 16th century in order to fit in both with the adjacent chapel and with the magnificent painted glass which filled both sets of windows. At the west end of the main chapel, there was a tower and doorway of which fragments still survive. Sandys' chantry consisted of a rectangular structure with a polygonal east end and a small tower at its south-west corner. The new building was of brick construction with ashlar facing. It seems to have possessed an elaborate vault with extensive painted bosses.[41] Even today the ruins remind us of the expensive external decoration with the canopied and decorated niches, and with the family heraldry, of Bray and Sandys, that adorned the upper parts of the walls (Fig. 22).

The chantry and its lands were dissolved in 1547, but restored by Queen Mary in 1558 when the priest was given the responsibility of being school master (see above), and this continued under Elizabeth. The buildings were now divided into a religious part and a schoolroom in the nave, to which was subsequently added a schoolmaster's

36   On the glass see H. Wayment, 'The stained glass of the Chapel of the Holy Ghost, Basingstoke', *Archaeologia* 107 (1982), 141–51; A. Smith, '"As my lord of Winchester shall devise"', 48–52.

37   Wayment, 'Stained glass', 143.

38   Much of the glass is still viewable at the nearby Vyne, which is now the property of the National Trust.

39   Wayment, 'Stained glass', 145.

40   Howard and Wilson, *The Vyne*, 42, 47–51, 54–6; Baigent & Millard, *Basingstoke*, 692–3.

41   Baigent & Millard, *Basingstoke*, 111–12, quoting Camden at the end of the 16th century.

house. The accounts show a clear distinction in the accountants' minds between chapel, in which leading figures continued to be buried, and the school room. They also record repairs to the building including frequent references to expenditure on a glazier for work on the windows, suggesting the need for maintenance of the great chapel windows.[42] A succession of the town's elite chose to be buried in the chapel here.

The Hospital of St John the Baptist

This hospital was usually referred to as that of St John the Baptist, but occasionally to that of St Mary and St John the Baptist. It was founded or refounded by Walter of Merton (see above p. 3) in 1240–5 for elderly clergy and the poor, 'for the support of the ministers of the altar whose strength is failing and the wayfaring poor of Christ'.[43] He used, as an endowment, the land that he had inherited from his mother, and additional purchases were to be made by his executors. It also acquired land in the 13th century, from townsmen and from the abbot of Bromholm (Norf.) as well as from Walter himself.[44] In some cases, someone may have granted land in return for hospitality in old age, as with Thomas le Forester.[45] Moreover, in these early years, there are references to 'the warden, brothers and sisters of the hospital'.[46] The hospital was re-established on a firmer basis with royal protection and foundation by Henry III in 1262.[47] From 1270, it served as a rest home for sick fellows of Merton College.[48] There were occasional disputes as to who had the right of presentation to the head of the hospital.[49] In 1277, under Merton's will, the hospital's endowment was reinforced and provided for permanent chaplains. The hospital cultivated its lands directly until sometime after 1347, but from at least 1379 these were leased.[50] The lessee then had the house and chapel but had to maintain the chaplain and provide hospitality and accommodation for the warden of the College and for the sick fellows.[51] One episode gives an impression of a rather run down institution. A jury in 1401 stated that the warden of the hospital (of Merton College) was required to maintain a chaplain, a clerk and two poor people. For the last six years, no clerk or poor people had been provided for, while the warden had kept the revenues. For the next few

42 Millard, *Holy Ghost*, passim.
43 J.R.L. Highfield (ed.), *The Early Rolls of Merton College, Oxford* (Oxford Hist. Soc., 1964).
44 See the deeds in Baigent & Millard, *Basingstoke*, 593–609. The grant from Bromholm abbey, represented a bequest of land in Basyng from William St John, the lord there, and the grant to the hospital may have been a sensible rationalisation of resources by the abbey.
45 Baigent & Millard, *Basingstoke*, 598, see above, 57.
46 Baigent & Millard, *Basingstoke*, 597.
47 J.R.L. Highfield (ed.), *Early Rolls of Merton College, Oxford*, 21, 50–1; *Cal. Chart.* II, 44.
48 Baigent & Millard, *Basingstoke*, 610; Highfield, *Early Rolls of Merton*, 51; *ODNB*, s.v., Merton, Walter of (*c.*1205–77), administrator, Bishop of Rochester, and founder of Merton College, Oxford (accessed 11 Jan. 2017).
49 *Cal. Pat.* 1343–1345, 258, 308; *Cal. Fine* XII, 1399–1405, 240–1.
50 Merton Coll., 4356; Baigent & Millard, *Basingstoke*, 614.
51 Baigent & Millard, *Basingstoke*, 615; H.E. Salter (ed.), *Registrum annalium collegii Mertoniensis, 1403–1521* (Oxford Hist. Soc., 1923), 268.

years the crown confiscated the revenues and payments to the warden of Merton were not resumed until 1405.[52] In some cases it also provided corrodies or pensions.[53]

Nothing survives of the hospital buildings, which lay to the north of the river Loddon. There are scattered references to them in the documents: the tiled roof of the chapel, the hall with a new chimney, with a new bay window in 1495 and a chamber, and a new barn.[54] In 1697, there survived a chief house and a house for the sick fellows, as well as a sort of chapel in which there was preaching once a month.[55] Letters at the end of the 18th century refer to the chapel as a flint building with gothic windows, stone mullions and quoins, but by then bricked up. Later it was recorded that the roof had a semi-circular timber roof with carved bosses, and that it was about twelve feet long and five feet broad. This seems very small and raises the question of whether this might have been a grand chamber for the Master rather than the chapel, particularly since other references show that the latter was able to be used for preaching and that it had a separate chancel.[56] By then (1752) the building had been divided into two floors creating a bedroom above. [57] A pamphlet of 1808 suggests the presence of flint buildings whose appearance had been much destroyed by a modern building of brick.[58]

Religious Life During the Reformations of the 16th Century

The 16th century was a time of immense change and fluctuations in religious life and attitudes, better known as 'the Reformation'. Government policy changed on several occasions: the break with Rome under Henry VIII, the Protestant reformation of Edward VI, the return to Rome under Mary and the establishment of a broader Protestant settlement under Elizabeth. Successive changes were met with varying degrees of enthusiasm, opposition or indifference by the townsmen. We can see something of the changing attitudes, as mediated through the views of the vicar, in the wills of the townsmen.

The evidence suggests that on the eve of the Henrician Reformation many citizens possessed an enthusiasm for the traditional religious ideas. The parish church today gives us a clear sense of the grand aspirations of the town's parishioners, reinforced by the rebuilding at the Holy Ghost chapel. But the former's internal appearance before the Reformation would have been very different from what we see now. This was a church and a world full of different altars where masses were being said for the citizens of the town, and statues and lights were maintained in honour of individual saints. Something of this world can be seen in contemporary wills, such as that of William Stocker in 1503. He was to be buried in the chapel of the Holy Ghost in Basingstoke. Most of his bequests, however, were to the main parish church 'also I bequeath to the light of the holy cross in

---

52   Baigent & Millard, *Basingstoke*, 51.
53   Baigent & Millard, *Basingstoke*, 255–6.
54   Baigent & Millard, *Basingstoke*, 643–45; Merton Coll., 4363.
55   Baigent & Millard, *Basingstoke*, 648.
56   Baigent & Millard, *Basingstoke*, 648.
57   Baigent & Millard, *Basingstoke*, 650.
58   J. Jefferson, *A Sketch of the History of Holy Ghost Chapel at Basingstoke* (Basingstoke, 1808), 9.

the church of Basingstoke, two sheep. To the light of the blessed Mary there, one sheep. To the chapel of St Thomas the bishop there, one sheep. To the repairs of the Church of Basingstoke, 6*s.* 8*d.*, and to the repairs of the chapel of the Holy Ghost, 3*s.* 4*d.*'.[59] Bequests for the saying of masses and to the saints and the holy company of heaven were a regular feature of their wills.[60]

The dramatic changes of the Henrician Reformation made an impact on Basingstoke. There were attacks on images. Lord Sandys was asked to send a particular image to Thomas Cromwell in London in 1538.[61] He did so. Between 1537 and 1547 if the church possessed a doom painting over the chancel arch this would have been removed and the wall was painted white with decorated Tudor rose and Prince of Wales feathers.[62] But building works continued to be carried out in 1540 with a new porch. Edward's reign saw further change, of which the most notable was probably the closure of the Holy Ghost chantry and the introduction of successive Protestant prayer books, but few wills survive from this period.

The accession of Mary allowed for the return of traditional religion, and this had some impact, as seen in the clauses of the wills granting the testator's soul to Christ, the Virgin Mary and the company of saints.[63] Town leaders took the opportunity to recover the lands of the Holy Ghost chapel, previously confiscated under Edward VI. Thereafter, it remained a combination of a chapel, in which distinguished members of the town continued to be buried, a social meeting place, and a school. The records of the guild provide a sense of what needed to be spent and done to achieve this refoundation, and of the readiness to pay to restore the old institutions. Altogether 94 townsfolk contributed to an initial fund.[64] Its existence and its land had to be recovered, culminating in the expensive authorisation with the Great Seal of England.[65] There was money to be spent on embellishment and repair, including the expenses for an alderman and a warden going to London to obtain bricks from the neighbouring Marquis of Winchester, presumably from the surplus of his building works at Basing. Then there were the expenses for the internal refitting to make the church ready for Catholic worship: a joiner for making an image, painting the image and the rood, a Holy water pot, sawing rails for the chapel, and carpentry in the chancel, the purchase of an organ, and wax for candles.[66] New vestments and internal fittings were needed such as the altar hangings with embroidered silk and embroidered velvet which in 1561 were in the custody of Agnes Yate.[67] The will of John Ronanger drawn up in 1558, at the end of Mary's reign, shows something of the uncertainty of these years. His bequests suggest a conservative Catholic set of views. He left £20 for a silver cross for the church at all times when needed, but it was to remain in the custody of two fellow citizens, and £2 for a bell in the church tower. He left a white suit of vestments for the use of the church to his two daughters (one of

59   Baigent & Millard, *Basingstoke*, 30 (the present location of this will is unknown).
60   e.g. HRO, 1513B/1; 1520B/9; 1534B/34; 1536B/13; 1540B/35; 1544B/110; 1537U/089.
61   *L & P Hen VIII*, XIII(2), 102.
62   A painting of this was displayed in the north-east chapel in 2017.
63   HRO, 1554B/110; 1555U/11; 1557U/089; 1557U/230.
64   Millard, *Holy Ghost*, 1–4.
65   Millard, *Holy Ghost*, 1–10.
66   Millard, *Holy Ghost*, 7.
67   Millard, *Holy Ghost*, 15.

whom was Agnes Yate) until the last of them died.[68] That he did not make a straight gift to the church suggests the uncertainties, and fears that further religious change might occur.

Under Elizabeth, the royal supremacy over the church was re-established, as were many Protestant ideas including changing ideas of salvation. The saints ceased to be a feature in will bequests.[69] One relic of Elizabethan change was the return to the parish church of the royal arms, the symbol of the royal supremacy, which survive from 1596. But at the beginning of the reign, there seemed no reason why the return of Protestantism should be any more permanent than the short-lived changes of Catholic Mary. As we have seen, the altar hangings of the Holy Ghost chapel were retained in private hands. These had presumably ceased to be used, but precautions were made being in the belief that government policy might change yet again. The ideas of the townsmen did not all change overnight. By contrast some early Elizabethan wills include reference to the traditional ideas of the company of saints, as with that of Margaret Halle in 1560.[70] A new bell was installed in 1561–2.[71]

68   HRO, 1558B 1999/1.
69   e.g. 1570B/156; 1571B/193; 1574B/136; 1575B/44; 1574B/177; 1576B/093; 1580B/99; 1581B/111; TNA, PROB 11/66/131.
70   HRO, 21M65/D2/13.
71   Millard, *Holy Ghost*, 18–20.

Basingstoke After 1600

BASINGSTOKE IN THE 16th century had been at the peak of its importance. Its subsequent developments are being examined more thoroughly and reveal a dynamic picture of growth and difficulty, and of change and continuity. Here, prior to future publication, it seems worth sketching some of the key later developments that have helped to make the modern town so different from the world that we have been examining.[1] By 1600, the town had already acquired three major functions: as a market centre for the surrounding area of north-east Hampshire and beyond; as a stopping point on the main route from London to the west, to Andover, Salisbury and beyond; and as a major industrial centre.

In the 17th and 18th centuries, the town suffered particularly from its industrial difficulties. The cloth industry dominated in the early part of the 17th century and it continued on a much smaller scale as a producer of poor quality cloth. But the town retained its other two major functions. It remained a key place on the route to the west and its inns and related occupations continued to flourish and benefit from the coaches and carts which travelled through the town. Moreover, it retained its role as a market town for the area beyond. This can be seen in the letters of a rector's daughter of Steventon, eight miles away. When Jane Austen wanted ink and drawing paper, it was to Basingstoke that she came. When her father bought a new desk or a new bed, it was to a craftsman in the town that he came. Here was the local doctor or the public dance.[2] When the canal was built to Basingstoke in 1794, it reflected a sense that the town remained a marketing centre for the area around, whether for exporting grain or importing coal. Nevertheless, this was a time when Basingstoke must have seemed increasingly in the doldrums.

In the 19th century, the fortunes of the town were transformed by the coming of the railways and by a group of 19th century religious nonconformists and entrepreneurs. Between 1839 and 1860 Basingstoke's potential was enormously enhanced as it became a major railway hub with access to London (1839), Southampton (1840), Reading (1848) and Exeter (1860). It should be noted that Reading gave it access to the industrial areas of the north for coal, iron and textiles as well as new markets. Moreover, a group of men now emerged who transformed the potential for growth into growth itself. The Quakers Richard Wallis and Charles Steevens transformed a local agricultural machinery firm into a major business producing threshing machines, traction engines, wagons and steam rollers, and sold their products both in Britain and around the world. The Baptist

---

1   For further details see the full text on the Hampshire VCH work in progress: https://www. victoriacountyhistory.ac.uk/counties/hampshire/work-in-progress (accessed 10 Jan. 2017).

2   *Steventon*, 61–4.

Thomas Burberry and his Congregationalist associates developed a succession of three different companies and three different factories producing clothes manufactured from northern textiles. These were distributed around the world with the last of these companies, still named after Burberry, remaining a major international fashion house. The result of this renewed period of industrial expansion was that between 1861 and 1901 the population of the town doubled.

In the 20th century, important new light engineering and chemical industries, developed, and major national shopping chains arrived, but by 1950s the town was arguably in decline. The key transformation occurred in the 1960s, with the conscious attempt at expansion, initially backed by London overspill, when the town took on the familiar shape of today. Much of the core of the old town was swept away, to make room for a large shopping centre, subsequently further enlarged, a reminder that throughout its history, a key function of the town has been as a marketing centre for the area around. Old factories were closed or moved out and have been demolished or redeveloped. New office blocks reflect the shift from an industrial town to a commercial role. Housing estates have proliferated. The motorway and the ring road have become familiar. Basingstoke is now a thoroughly modern town, but with a long and distinguished history that is all too often forgotten.

a.	acre
Baigent & Millard, *Basingstoke*	F.J. Baigent and J.E. Millard, *A history of the ancient town and manor of Basingstoke in the county of Southampton...* (Basingstoke & London, 1889)
BL	British Library
Cal. Chart.	*Calendar of the Charter Rolls preserved in the Public Record Office* (HMSO, 1903–27)
Cal. Fine	*Calendar of the Fine Rolls preserved in the Public Record Office* (HMSO, 1911–62)
Cal. Inq. Misc	*Calendar Inquisitions Miscellaneous (Chancery) preserved in the Public Record Office* (HMSO, 1916–2003)
Cal. Inq. Post Mortem	*Calendar Inquisitions post mortem preserved in the Public Record Office* (HMSO, 1904–2010)
Cal. Lib.	*Calendar of the Liberate Rolls preserved in the Public Record Office* (HMSO, 1916–64)
Cal. Pat.	*Calendar of Patent Rolls preserved in the Public Record Office* (HMSO, 1891–1986)
CUHB	D.M. Palliser (ed.), *The Cambridge Urban History of Britain*, vol. 1, 650–1540 (Cambridge, 2000)
C.U.L.	Cambridge University Library
Dioc. Pop. Retns	A. Dyer and D.M. Palliser (eds), *Diocesan Population Returns for 1563 and 1603* (Records of Social and Economic History, n.s. 31, 2005)
Domesday	A. Williams and G.H. Martin, *Domesday Book: a complete translation* (London, 2002)
Emden, *OU Reg. to 1500;*	A.B. Emden, *A Biographical Register of the University of Oxford to AD 1500* (Oxford, 1957–9)
Emden, *OU Reg. 1501 to 1540*	A.B. Emden, *A Biographical Register of the University of Oxford AD 1501–1540* (Oxford, 1974)
Glasscock (ed.), *Subsidy 1334*	R.E. Glasscock (ed.), *The Lay Subsidy of 1334* (Records of Social and Economic History, n.s. 2, 1975)
English Inland Trade	M. Hicks (ed.), *English Inland Trade, 1430–1540* (Oxford, 2015)

Hants Tax List 1327	P. Mitchell-Fox and M. Page (eds), *The Hampshire tax list of 1327*, HR Ser. 20 (2014)
HFC	*Hampshire Field Club*
Himsworth, *Winchester Coll.*	S. Himsworth, *Winchester College Muniments*, 3 vols (Chichester, 1976–84)
HRO	Hampshire Record Office
HR Ser.	Hampshire Record Series
HR Soc.	Hampshire Record Society
Hare, *Prospering Society*	J. Hare, *A Prospering Society: Wiltshire in the Later Middle Ages* (Hertford, 2011)
Hare, 'Regional Prosperity'	J. Hare, 'Regional prosperity in fifteenth-century England: some evidence from Wessex', in M.A. Hicks (ed.), *Revolution and Consumption in Late Medieval England* (Woodbridge, 2001)
Keene, *Medieval Winchester*	D. Keene, *A Survey of Medieval Winchester* (Oxford, 1985)
L & P Hen. VIII	*Letters and Papers, Foreign and Domestic, of the Reign of Henry VIII* (HMSO, 1864–1932)
Macray, *Selborne*	W.D. Macray (ed.), *Calendar of charters and document relating to Selborne and its priory*, preserved in the 2 vols (1891–4)
Mag. Coll.	Archives of Magdalen College, Oxford
Merton Coll.	Merton College Records, Oxford
Mapledurwell	J. Hare, J. Morrin and S. Waight, *Mapledurwell* (2012)
Millard, *Holy Ghost*	J.E. Millard (ed.), *Book of accounts of the wardens of the fraternity of the Holy Ghost in Basingstoke, 1557–1664* (1882)
NHL	National Heritage List for England: http://www.historicengland.org.uk/listing/the-list
Pevsner, *North Hampshire*	M. Bullen, J. Crook, R. Hubbock and N. Pevsner, *Hampshire: Winchester and the North* (New Haven and London, 2010)
ODNB	*Oxford Dictionary of National Biography*: http://www.oxforddnb.com
Overland Trade Database	http://www.overlandtrade.org
PHFC	*Proceedings of Hampshire Field Club and Archaeological Society* (now *Hampshire Studies*)
Pipe R	*Pipe Roll*
PRS	Pipe Roll Society

Reg. Distr. Wealth 1524–5 J. Sheail (ed. R.W. Hoyle), *The Regional Distribution of Wealth in England as indicated in the 1524/5 lay subsidy returns* (List and Index Society, special series, 29, 1998)

Roberts, *Hampshire Houses* E. Roberts, *Hampshire Houses, 1250–1700: their dating and development* (Winchester, 2003: new edition with extra chapter, 2016)

Rosen, 'Winchester in transition' A. Rosen, 'Winchester in transition, 1580–1700' in P. Clark (ed.), *County Towns in Pre-industrial England* (1981)

SAO Southampton Archives Office

Steventon J. Morrin, *Steventon* (2016)

TNA The National Archives, Kew

VCH Hants *The Victoria County History of the Counties of England: Hampshire and the Isle of Wight* (1902–11)

WCM Winchester College Muniments, Winchester College

GLOSSARY

Advowson: the right to choose the candidate as rector or vicar to a church or chapel

Appropriation: the grant of the property of a church (land and tithes) to a monastery or other religious house.

Assize: a series of trading regulations particularly referring to bread and ale, but extended at Basingstoke to cover a wide range of occupations. Effectively a tax on pursuing an occupation.

Aulnage: a national tax on marketed cloth. The surviving detailed records are extremely scanty.

Brokage Book: books recording the duty (brokage) on goods sent inland from the port of Southampton.

Chantry: an endowment to provide for the saying of masses for the soul of the donor and other specified people.

Chapel: a subsidiary church within the parish, or part of a church incorporating an extra side-altar.

Clothier: an entrepreneur involved in the large-scale production and marketing of cloth.

Demesne: the land cultivated directly by the lord. Usually leased out to a tenant in the later Middle Ages.

Estreat: a summary of the fines imposed by the court.

Feoffee: a trustee granted land as a means of the owner passing on the land to the personal or institutional beneficiary.

Fuller: once cloth had been woven, it was fulled whereby the rough surface of the woven cloth was transformed to the smooth surface of the finished marketable cloth. The fuller was initially a craftsman practising this particular part of the manufacturing process, but often became, as at Basingstoke, an entrepreneur engaged in linking together the various stages of the manufacturing and marketing process.

Hayward: the elected manorial official responsible for the maintenance of the common rights of tenants and lords on the meadow and on the common fields.

Hundred: a sub-division of the county from before the Norman Conquest and nominally containing 100 hides. Here it comprised Basingstoke and the surrounding villages. At Basingstoke, the hundred court was the town court held every three weeks.

Inquisition post mortem: an enquiry to establish what lands and rights were held of the king by the dead person.

Inventories: here refers to the inventories of goods drawn up after death as part of the probate proceedings, here found in the 16th century.

Manor: a landed estate originally held in return for military service, and usually incorporating demesne, tenants and right to hold a court.

Parish: the area attached to a parish church, in this case Basing, Basingstoke and Up Nately, all belonging to a united parish headed by Basing and then Basingstoke.

Pipe roll: a) records of receipts and expenditure of the royal exchequer or b) in relation to the bishops of Winchester, the estate records, incorporating the manorial records of each of manors of the bishop.

Rectory: a church living served by a rector, who generally received the full income of land, tithes and offerings in the church. As in Basing, the rectory might be granted to a religious house, with the parish work being carried out by a vicar.

Stint: pasturing rights for a specified number of livestock on the common land attached to a tenancy.

Rood: the image of the crucifixion displayed within the church.

Subsidy: the lay subsidy was a royal tax upon the laity. In the town it was usually assessed ion the value of moveable goods.

View of frankpledge: the court held at Basingstoke twice a year, for the town and the parishes of the hundred.

Vicar: a priest or clerk serving a church or parish where most of the tithes and land had been granted to a monastery or other religious body.

YEAR		1399	1409	1415	1422	1429	1437	1444	1454	1455	1464	1470	1478
Victuals	bakers	2	1	3	2	1	2	3	2	2	2	2	3
	brewers & tapsters	39	40	35							34		
	brewers				34	24	22	28	17	19		24	21
	tapsters				4	10	21	29	11	11		18	14
	butcher	1	3	5	5	4	3	2	4	4	3	4	3
	fishmonger	1	3	6	3	1	1	2	2	2	1	1	2
	inn-keeper	4	3	3	4	3	3	3	4	3	3	3	3
	millers	3	2	2	3	3	3	3	2	2	4	3	4
	Sub-total	50	52	54	55	46	55	67	40	43	47	55	50
Mercantile	grocers										6		
	mercers			1	1						2	6	2
	drapers											2	2
	clothiers												
	Sub-total			1	1						8	8	4
Textiles	dyers								1		5	1	1
	fullers							2	1	1	4	2	6
	weavers	2	3	1		2	3	5	3	4	5	8	7
	Sub-total cloth	2	3	1	0	2	3	7	5	5	14	11	14
	Sub-total and mercantile	2	3	2	1	2	3	7	5	5	22	19	22
Leather	cobbler		5	3	2	3	1	2	2	2		2	2
	tanner		1	1		1	1	1	1	1		1	2
	glover												
	saddler							1	1	1		1	1
	pelterer		1			1						1	
	Sub-total		7	4	2	4	3	4	4	4	5	5	5
Clothing	cap-maker											1	
	hosier												
	tailor		5	5	4	3	2	3	3	3	3	5	7
	Sub-total	11	5	5	4	3	2	3	3	3	5	6	7
Metal	smith		2	3	4	2	3		2	2	2	2	2
	brasier										1	1	
	ironmonger										1	1	
	Sub-total	3	2	3	3	2	3		2	2	4	4	2
Building	carpenter		2	5	5	3	8	7*	4*	3	3	3	2
	mason			1							2	2	3
	tiler									1	1	1	
	Sub-total		2	5	6	3	8	7	4	4	6	6	5
Wood	cooper										1	1	
	wheelwright												
	joiner										1	2	
	Sub-total			0		0					2	3	3
Others	fletcher				1							1	
	chandler						2				1	1	2
	barber											2	2
	Sub-total	5		0	1	0	2			1	4	4	4
Labourers & journeymen		7	7	13	9	7	9	6	8	4	2	13	16
Total		78	78	86	81	67	85	94	66	68	98	115	111

Sources: HRO 148/M71/2/1/10, 2/1/15, 2/7/1, 2/1/26, 2/7/2, 2/1/47, 2/7/4, 2/7/5, 2/1/63, 2/7/7, 2/7/8, 2/7/9, 2/7/12, 2/7/14, 2/7/16, 2/1/65, 2/7/17, 2/7/18, 2/7/19, 2/7/20, 2/1/67, 2/7/21, 2/7/22, 2/7/27, 2/7/30, 2/7/31, 2/7/34, 2/7/35.

Notes: # bakers and brewers * includes sawyers

1491	1499	1501	1503	1512	1516	1524	1530	1531	1535	1539	1540	1546	1552	1554	1558	1562	1583
4	4	6	6	7	7	4	4	5	6	5	5	4	17#	19	5	5	4
11	7	4	6	7	4	9	4	4	10	9	7	5			13	12	5
26	14	16	16	19	24	23	27	30	17		11	5					7
4	3	3	3	2	2	2	2	2	2	4	4	2	4	4	3	4	5
4	4	4	5	5	6	2	4	4	2	3	3	4	5	3	2	4	
3	4	4	3	5	4	4	4	4	3	3	3	3	3	3	4	4	
5	5	5	5	6	4	4	4	4	3	3	3	3		4	3	3	3
57	41	37	44	51	51	48	49	53	37	27	36	26	29	33	30	27	24
7	6	4	5	5	6	3	5	6	3	5	5	5	7	6	6	6	4
2	4	7	6	6	5	5	6	8	10	9	9	8	5	6		9	
								14	15	13	9	5			7		4
9	10	11	11	11	11	8	11	28	28	27	23	18	12	12	13	15	8
4	2	2	2	3	4	5	3	3	3	3	3	3	1	4	4	4	0
10	12	13	15	19	25	31	33	30	10								
5	8	8	13	17	15	23	16	19	15							3	0
19	22	23	30	39	44	59	52	52	28	3	3	3	1	4	4	7	0
28	32	34	41	51	55	64	63	66	56	30	26	21	13	16	17	22	8
3	3	3	3	4	4	4	4	3	3	5	5	5	2	8	6	6	5
	2									1		3	1	2		2	1
1	2	2	2	1	2	2	3	3	2	3	3	3	3	4	2	4	
2	2	1	1	2	2	2	3	3	2	2	1	2	3	3	3	3	
	1																
6	9	7	6	7	8	8	10	9	7	11	9	10	9	17	12	15	6
			1													1	
5	3	4	6	4	7	7	6	5	5	8				4	6	8	8
5	3	4	6	4	8	7	6	5	5	8				4	6	9	8
2	2	2	3	3	3	3		3	3	1	2		4	4	4	4	
										1 cut	2 cut			2		2	
2	2	2	3	3	3	3		3	3	2	4		4	6	4	6	
						2		1							1		
			1														
			2	1												1	
			3	3		1									1	1	
		1		1											1	1	
1	1														3		
			2												2		
1	1		1	2	1										6	1	
1				1													
2						1	2	2	2	2	2	3		3	3		1
2	2	2	2	2	4	5	2	3	3	3	3	3		3	3	3	
5	2	2	2	2	5	6	4	5	5	5	5	6		6	6	3	1
17	12	14	12	21	24	16		14	9	9	11	3			6	7	
121	102	100	115	141	158	155	132	156	122	92	91	66	55	89	81	91	47

INDEX

CPSIA information can be obtained
at www.ICGtesting.com
Printed in the USA
JSHW022225211219
3115JS00002B/16